ULTIMATE GOLF POINTERS

FROM BEGINNER TO WINNER!

Ron Strickland

Archway Publishing books may be ordered through booksellers or by contacting:

Archway Publishing
1663 Liberty Drive
Bloomington, IN 47403
www.archwaypublishing.com
844-669-3957

Interior Image Credit: Bram Hagen, Lisa Strickland

ISBN: 978-1-6657-1909-4 (sc)
ISBN: 978-1-6657-1908-7 (e)

Library of Congress Control Number: 2022903215

Print information available on the last page.

Archway Publishing rev. date: 5/5/2022

CONTENTS

ACKNOWLEDGMENTS

I would like to thank my uncle, Billy Elmore, for introducing me to the game of golf. I would like to thank Tiger Woods for showing the world what a golf game could look like.

I would like to thank my dear friend Bram Hagen for his outstanding work on the book cover and the "Ball Flight Laws Diagram." What an awesome job on both!

I would like to recognize and thank my darling (and beautiful) wife, Lisa, for everything she did in contributing to this book. She provided the drawings, the editing, and the computer expertise, and she also knew enough about the game of golf to call my hand when I did not make a pointer clear enough. Great job!

I would also like to thank my family, friends, and golfing buddies for all of their support and encouragement during the long process of writing this book. What a great group of people. To my golfing buddies—thanks for all the fun we called research!

To all of you, I am very grateful. Thank you! Thank you! Thank you!

Sincerely,

Ron Strickland

PREFACE

I am writing this book in an effort to reach three distinct groups of people. The first group I am trying to reach is the individuals who have never played the game of golf. The second group is those who have played the game of golf for some time yet still somewhat struggle with their game. The third group is anyone who is associated with the golf industry and/or anyone who would love to see their business and community grow/prosper.

Group 1

In this group are the individuals who have never played the game of golf for one reason or another. Maybe they have just never been around anyone who played the game so they had no earthly idea where to start. Maybe they have always heard that it is an expensive game and they didn't know whether they wanted to make an investment in something they might not even like. Maybe they are just a little uncomfortable going out and trying something new by themselves. I, personally, can fully understand all of these maybes because at one time or another, I had them all myself. I would like to start out by addressing these maybes.

Maybe #1, as to where to start? Why not check around with your family, friends, co-workers, or fellow church members to see how many of them play golf. Maybe they would be willing to help you get started in the game. If not, just go to your nearest public golf course and introduce yourself. I guarantee you the owner/manager will be more than glad to help you get started.

Maybe #2, as to the expense of the game? If you will take the time to read Chapter 1: Getting Started, I believe that you will be amazed at how reasonable the game of golf can be. You can probably get your hands on a set of used clubs for close to nothing, and it doesn't cost you a cent to practice golf. Usually the more you practice, the better you get. Another good thing about practicing golf is that you can do it for hours on end or for ten to fifteen minutes at a time. What a cool option!

Maybe #3, going out and trying something new by yourself? See the response to Maybe #1.

While speaking with individuals who had never played the game of golf, I came across some more concerns:

1. If I wanted to play golf, how would I get my hands on some clubs?
2. What clubs would I need?
3. How in the world would I ever hit that little ball with those big, long clubs?
4. What else would I need other than golf balls and golf clubs?
5. What else would I need to know before playing so that I would not embarrass myself or accidentally kill someone?

For the answer:

- To Question 1, see Chapter 1: Getting Started.
- To Question 2, see Chapter 9: Club Selection.
- To Question 3, see Chapter 3: Grip, Chapter 4: Setup, Chapter 6: The Golf Swing, and Chapter 7: The Golf Swing (Broken Down).
- To Question 4, see Chapter 1: Getting Started.
- To the first part of Question 5, see Chapter 22: Golf Etiquette.
- To the second part of Question 5, see the rest of this book.

Group 2

If you have been playing golf for a while but still somewhat struggle with your game, please take the time to read this book because there are numerous pointers here that can positively impact your game. Furthermore, most of these pointers can impact your game overnight. For an idea about what is covered in this book, take a close look at the Table of Contents.

Group 3

If you are associated with the golf industry or are just an individual who would love to see your business and community grow/prosper, I believe that you, too, can greatly benefit from this book, by not only reading it, but by sharing it with everyone in your community. I firmly believe that this book has the potential to grow the game of golf by growing the number of new participants as well as growing the skill level of all current golfers. Along with this increased skill level usually comes more play. More play, whether it is from new golfers or from increased rounds by current, regenerated golfers, equals more profit. More profit equals more desirable neighborhoods. More desirable neighborhoods equal better schools. Better schools equal, well, I believe you get the point. In my book, or perhaps because of my book—and your willingness to share it with your community—what a win-win situation. Not only does the game grow but so does your community and business.

Note: If you don't believe that this book has the potential to grow the number of new participants and/or the skill level of all current golfers, I challenge you to turn to any chapter in this book and spend two to three minutes glancing over the material. Go ahead—I dare you!

Thank you in advance for taking the time to read and/or share this book.

With great appreciation,

Ron Strickland

INTRODUCTION

Welcome to what may well be the best golf instruction book ever written, for this book will take you from beginner to winner. Not only will this book take you from beginner to winner, but it will also help you anywhere along the way, from beginner to winner!

In this book, rather than having you look through hundreds of pages of pictures, humor, and golf pointers, I have tried to cover all aspects of the game in a direct and precise way. For those of you who learn best through pictures, I suggest the following: Each time you read one of the pointers in this book and need further clarification, simply google that subject and then you can look at as many pictures as you like. Study those pictures, along with the pointer, and once you feel that you have a pretty good understanding of that pointer, move on to the next pointer in this book.

If you are going to need to google pictures to help you with these golf pointers, why do you need this book, you may ask. In my humble opinion, you need this book because it contains the pointers that you need in the order that you need them. In addition, I have included a vast amount of golf wisdom, golf principles, and general thoughts on golf—information that you could spend years gathering. Believe me, that is how long it has taken me to gather and organize this information.

For those of you who, at first glance, think that this is too much information, please know that I have put all of this information together because I know that not everyone has the disposition, time, or money to attend full-scale golf clinics. This book may be the only way that a lot of people can get their hands on this information. By having access to the information in this book, you can study and/or practice golf any time you like and/or any time you have time available. I truly believe that is an awesome deal for everyone!

To get the best and quickest results out of this book, do the following:

- First, check out the Table of Contents to get an overview of what this book offers.
- Second, glance through any of the chapters to get a feel for the book.
- Third, start back anywhere in the book that you think would do you and your golf game the most good. If you want some cool, yet practical, ways of looking at the golf swing, see Chapter 6: The Golf Swing. For great drawings regarding the fundamentals of golf, see Chapter 8: Drawings. If you want specific pointers for hitting the different clubs, see Chapter 11: Hitting Different Clubs. If you want

information on how to hit specialty shots, see Chapter 12: Hitting Specialty Shots. For information on how to hit from uneven lies, see Chapter 13: Hitting from Uneven Lies. For pointers on how to escape bunkers, see Chapter 14: Hitting from Fairway Bunkers, and Chapter 15: Hitting from Greenside Bunkers. If you just want general, yet valuable, golf pointers, see Chapter 17: Golf Wisdom. If you want information on how to get more distance (and who doesn't?), see Chapter 18: How to Get More Distance. For great thoughts and drills regarding practicing, see Chapter 19: Practice Thoughts and Drills.

- If you are a beginner golfer, I strongly recommend that you start at the beginning of the book and work your way through it. If you come across a term and/or jargon you are not familiar with, look it up in the Glossary, which is located at the back of this book. If the Glossary does not fully explain the term and/or jargon to your satisfaction, google it, because the better you understand the terms and jargon, the faster you will learn the game.

- If you are a golfer who has been playing for many years but still tends to somewhat struggle with your game, I highly recommend that you, too, start at the beginning of the book and work your way through it. I cover a lot of things in this book that you may have known in the past but may not have thought about in a while.

- No matter where you are in your game, I suggest that when you are looking through this book, you use a pen and notepad to jot down any pointers, principles, and/or wisdom that jump out at you. Put these pointers, principles, and wisdom into your own "mini-book" so that you can readily get to them. If you prefer, use your smartphone or any other electronic gadget you have available.

- Next, I suggest that you take this book and/or your "mini-book" with you when you go to practice golf or when you have a few minutes to study golf.

- In addition, I suggest that you put key pointers and/or thoughts on index cards or your smartphone so that you can refer to them when you play. Having a few pointers with you to jog your memory can truly make a difference in your game. You may want to have a few key pointers regarding how to hit the different clubs, how to hit specialty shots, or how to hit from uneven lies. Maybe you want a few key pointers for how to hit from the different lies in greenside bunkers? By all means, note the pointers that mean the most to you at that point in time.

Beginner golfers who follow these suggestions will be blown away by how quickly they pick up the game of golf. Seasoned, yet sometimes struggling, golfers who follow these suggestions will be amazed at how quickly their game improves.

For those golfers who are afraid that using index cards will slow down the game, please relax. I have found that they actually do the opposite—they speed up the game. By having the cards organized and in a specific order, the beginner golfer can hit one good shot for a given distance rather than three or more not-so-good shots. Hitting fewer shots and not having to look for wayward shots—certainly sounds like a timesaver to me!

<u>In Case of Emergency</u>

If you are a beginner golfer and absolutely must play golf tomorrow (family reunion, business outing, fundraiser, etc.), see Chapter 21: Quick Pointers. The thoughts and pointers in that chapter will not be enough to make you a complete golfer but, hopefully, they will be enough to lead to an enjoyable round of golf.

In addition to checking out Chapter 21, please check out Chapter 22: Golf Etiquette. The thoughts and pointers found in that chapter should be enough to allow everyone around you the opportunity to have an enjoyable round of golf.

Once you get through your emergency, please pick back up at the beginning of this book. The information found in this book could change your life!

1

GETTING STARTED

Don't be overwhelmed by the amount of information in this book. You don't have to learn it all before you can play enjoyable golf. In fact, you don't have to learn it all before you can become a pretty good golfer. It has all been included so that you can take your game as far as you like. It has also all been included because a pointer that might not mean anything to you may be the very pointer that your golfing buddies need to take their game to the next level.

As a word of caution, consider the following:

- You don't have to use all the pointers in this book; use the ones that resonate with you. There are a lot of different ways to get the same results. Try the suggested ways and then choose the ones that work best for you.
- When practicing, practice one thing at a time, such as putting, chipping, pitching, hitting driver, hitting fairway woods/metals, hitting a fade, hitting a draw, etc. For thoughts and drills regarding practicing, see Chapter 19: Practice Thoughts and Drills.
- When practicing, take this book or your "mini-book" with you. Once you feel somewhat comfortable with one club or shot, move on to the next one.
- When practicing, please remember it has been said that probably the biggest difference between great golfers and struggling golfers is that great golfers practice the things they are not so good at, while struggling golfers continue practicing the things they are good at. So, if you want to become a great golfer, or at least see great improvement in your game, practice the things that you are not so good at.
- While you don't want a lot of thoughts running through your head when you are attempting to make a shot during a round of golf, you do want some thoughts running through your head when you are practicing. When practicing, if you

don't have any thoughts running through your head about how to hit the shot, you are probably just hitting balls. Just hitting balls is not the answer. In fact, if you are just hitting balls, you may be doing more harm than good because practice doesn't make perfect—practice makes permanent.

FIRST THINGS FIRST: STUDY, PRACTICE, PLAY

In golf, as in life, you should always do first things first. In golf, first things first means study, practice, and then play. If you don't do these three things in this order, you will forever hinder your progress.

Study

Study before you practice. If you don't study before you practice, how are you going to know what and how to practice? When it comes to studying, I am pretty much just talking about reading and taking notes. In my experience, you read to learn and you take notes to remember.

Practice

Practice before you play. When you practice, practice the correct things in the correct manner because practice makes permanent. For ideas on what and how to practice, see Chapter 19: Practice Thoughts and Drills. Please check out that chapter before ever playing!

Play

Sometime before you play, personalize your ball by marking it in some way. Marking your ball allows you to quickly identify it during play. Hitting the wrong ball can lead to penalties (and enemies)!

When playing, don't think about technique. Just visualize the shot. Your mind and body will make it happen. Visualize the trajectory, the carry (distance in air), and the roll.

When you first start playing, play from the correct tee boxes for your skill level and not your age. Once you have toned your game, you can move to the next tee boxes back, and so on. Most golf courses have four to five sets of tee boxes (for each hole). In the past, the tee box closest to the green was referred to as the "ladies' tee." In today's game, it is referred to more accurately as the "forward tee." The next tee box closest to the green is commonly referred to as the "seniors' tee." I believe that all beginner golfers, no matter their age, would enjoy the game more, and they would speed up their learning curve, if they chose to play from the forward or the second tee boxes closest to the greens until they developed their game. This would make the game a lot less frustrating for them and would greatly increase the speed of the game for everyone. What a win-win situation!

If you are a beginner golfer, please don't concern yourself too much with the rules of golf. You can learn and adhere to these once you have developed your game a bit. However, for everyone's sake, please familiarize yourself with proper golf etiquette. Practicing proper golf etiquette will allow everyone the opportunity to have an enjoyable round of golf. Please take the time to read Chapter 22: Golf Etiquette.

Here is some additional information for beginner golfers to consider:

- The lower the number on the club, the farther you should be able to hit the ball. In addition, most golfers can hit a wood/metal farther than an iron. See Chapter 9: Club Selection for specifics on each club.
- To help you determine which club to use for a particular shot, see Chapter 10: Pre-Shot Routine.
- Play each round as if it were a practice round. Don't worry about your score.
- When playing a round of golf with others, play the select-a-shot (scramble) format. The scramble format is a game in which two or more players tee off, pick the best shot, and then all play their next shot from within a club's length of that shot. The club length can't be any closer to the hole and the lie must be the same. In other words, if the shot selected was in a bunker, or in the rough, everyone must play from those same conditions. Every shot is conducted in that same manner until the ball has been holed. In the scramble format, no matter how new you are to the game, you can have a blast, because you don't have to hit a perfect shot every time. Hopefully, one of your teammates will make an excellent shot if you don't. If you are playing the scramble format with more experienced golfers, please abide by the rules of golf, if they choose to do so. You can lean on the more experienced golfers for guidance as to the rules.
- If you have trouble locating your ball after you have hit it, you may take a reasonable amount of time looking for it. This reasonable amount of time is negotiable. If there is a group right behind you, you may want to simply drop a ball where you think it should be and play on. Remember, you are playing the round as a practice round and not keeping an accurate score anyway. This philosophy makes the game a lot more enjoyable for everyone!
- In golf, you don't necessarily take turns hitting—whoever is farther away from the pin hits next. If someone else's ball is farther away from the pin, please remain behind them and not beside or in front of them, until after they have hit their

shot. No matter how good a golfer they may be, everyone hits a wayward shot now and then.

- If you hit a wayward shot, please yell "Fore" immediately for this gives everyone a "heads-up" to get their heads down.

- According to the rules of golf, the only time you can tee a ball up is when you are on the tee box. For that reason, most experienced golfers believe that you should take advantage of this every time, even if you are using an iron and teeing the ball at ground level. By using a tee, you ensure that the ball will not be sitting down. A ball sitting down is more difficult to hit.

- If using a tee when hitting a short iron from the tee box, swing down on the ball, breaking the tee each time. By breaking the tee you ensure that you definitely hit down on the ball. Hit the ball first and then take a divot on the target side of the ball. With short irons, your divot should start at the ball and should be about four inches long.

- Another bit of wisdom regarding the tee box: If you are trying to avoid trouble on one side or the other, tee up on the same side as the trouble and then simply aim and swing away from it.

- Since you are a beginner golfer and are playing each round as a practice round and not really concerning yourself with an accurate score, it is okay to better your lie so that you can make an easier and better shot. This too will speed up the game and will cut down on frustration for everyone. Only do this when you are playing by yourself or when your playing companions have agreed with this concept.

- When it comes to bettering your lie, if you are a beginner or senior golfer, you may even want to tee the ball up for all of your shots. It certainly makes the ball a lot easier to hit. A couple of senior golfing buddies of mine shared that is what they do and they have the time of their lives and don't have to worry about injuring themselves by striking the ground too harshly. (Thanks for sharing, JS and DG!)

- If you are a beginner golfer and are playing each round as a practice round, it is okay to toss your ball out of a bunker, if you have not had a chance to practice bunker shots. If you are playing with others, first ensure that they don't have a problem with you doing this.

- Once you have played enough practice rounds to feel somewhat comfortable on the course, get with the staff in the pro shop about getting a handicap established. Once you start playing to establish your handicap, you will need to play by the rules and you will need to play from the correct tee boxes. Get with someone from the pro shop for guidance on how to get a current copy of the rules and as to the appropriate tee boxes.

- By getting a handicap established, you will then be able to compete with any non-professional golfer on a level playing field. What a unique system and opportunity!

OBTAINING GOLF CLUBS

When you first start out in the game of golf, if you don't own a set of clubs don't despair for there are many ways you can get your hands on a set of golf clubs. First, most golf courses have clubs that you can rent for a reasonable fee. Second, you may be able to obtain reasonably priced clubs from garage sales, second-hand stores, friends, or neighbors. Before spending a lot of money on a new set of clubs, check around!

When you first start out, you truly don't need a whole set of clubs. A lot of good, if not great, golfers have started out playing rounds of golf with just a 3-wood/metal, 7-iron, and putter. By playing rounds of golf with nothing more than these three clubs, you will truly learn how to make golf shots. Making golf shots is what being a golfer is all about!

If you choose to go with new clubs, get with your local golf pro/vendor for guidance regarding:

- Length
- Lie Angle
- Shaft Flex*
- Grip Size
- Loft
- Weight
- How it looks and feels to you
- Forged, muscle-backed irons versus cavity-backed irons**

* Selecting the correct shaft flex can be somewhat important. If you usually hook the ball, a stiffer shaft may straighten your shots. If you slice the ball, a more flexible shaft may help you close the clubface at impact.

** Forged, muscle-backed irons are for good players. Cavity-backed (hollowed out in the back) irons are for beginner and intermediate golfers because they are more forgiving on mishits. For your information, even a lot of pros use cavity-backed irons.

Additional information regarding golf clubs: In a standard set of golf clubs, there is a half-inch difference in the length of each iron as well as with each wood. The higher the number, the shorter the club. The shorter the club, the closer you stand to the ball at address.

Before purchasing new clubs, inquire about getting club fitted. Getting club fitted can make a world of difference in your golf game.

If you have not been club fitted, ensure that your clubs are not too long for you. If the clubs are too long for you, you will likely bottom out during your downswing. Bottoming out will cost you distance and can even lead to injury. If your clubs are too long for you, simply grip down on them the needed amount so that you don't bottom out on the downswing. To determine whether your clubs are too long for you, see "Gripping the Club with the Lead Hand" in Chapter 3: Grip.

CHECKLIST OF ITEMS NEEDED FOR GOLF OUTING

- ❑ Collared shirt (most clubs/courses require them)
- ❑ Denim-free pants/shorts
- ❑ Golf clubs
- ❑ Golf balls – personalized/marked in some way
- ❑ Golf shoes
- ❑ Golf footies and/or socks
- ❑ Golf hat
- ❑ Golf glove(s)
- ❑ Golf towel(s)
- ❑ Golf tees (short and long)
- ❑ Ball mark repair tool
- ❑ Ball marker for marking your ball on the green
- ❑ Ball retriever
- ❑ Golf GPS and/or rangefinder
- ❑ Sunscreen
- ❑ Sunglasses
- ❑ Bug repellent
- ❑ Rain gear
- ❑ Large umbrella (for self)
- ❑ Small umbrella (for clubs)
- ❑ Cell phone
- ❑ Bluetooth speaker (optional)
- ❑ Medicine/bandages/fingernail clippers

You definitely don't need all of the items on this list to play a round of golf. I simply listed them all so that you could use it as a checklist. While golf shoes are nice, as a beginner golfer, you can get by using tennis shoes. In the long run, you will probably want to invest in a pair of golf shoes because they offer a lot better traction.

When it comes to footies or socks, the author always carries an extra pair in case he gets a hole in one. Get it? A hole-in-one, every golfer's dream!

When it comes to ball markers, it is always good to have an extra one in case you need to mark someone else's ball on the green as well as your own. Please don't mark their ball unless they ask you to—or if you receive their permission to do so.

When marking a ball on the green (marking where the ball is lying), place the marker directly behind the ball unless the ball marker will be in someone else's target line. If it will be in someone else's target line, mark the ball a clubhead or two over. However, when you go to make your putt, ensure that you move the ball back to its original lie.

If you are playing in the scramble format, you may want to mark to the side of the ball instead of directly behind it. This way no one has to putt over the marker.

2
CHAPTER

MINDSET

IN MY OPINION, YOUR MINDSET (ATTITUDE) IS THE MOST IMPORTANT THING IN GOLF because it is your mindset that separates you from all other golfers. It has been said that a bad attitude is worse than a bad golf swing. I believe that pretty much all of the golf experts would agree with that statement—they can fix your golf swing but only you can fix your attitude. To fix your attitude, read on!

Professional golfers have all kinds of coaches and hit thousands of balls a week, and they still hit bad shots sometimes. A beginner golfer, who may have never even hit a golf ball, makes one bad shot, and says, "I am no good at this game." That statement just doesn't make sense. What is even worse about that statement is that your subconscious mind hears and believes everything you say. So, if you want to be good at golf—or good at anything else in life for that matter—speak positively to yourself. Learn from what you do right and learn from what you do wrong. I assure you that if you will address golf, and life, with a fun-loving and learning attitude, you will have a blast and, over time, you will become quite good at both of them.

One of the things I love about the game of golf is that golf is a game you can play the rest of your life; all the time and energy you put into learning it will never be wasted. When it comes to golf, you never outgrow it and you never get too old for it. For ideas regarding never getting too old for it, revisit the scramble format idea shared in Chapter 1: Getting Started.

Another great thing I love about the game of golf is that you can play it by yourself. You never have to wait until someone else is in the mood and/or can find the time. Another great thing about the game of golf is that you never have to pass the ball. In golf, you get to make all the shots. What an awesome feeling!

Speaking of getting to make all the shots, one of the key things that I love to share with fellow golfers is that it is okay to hit a bad shot, just never hit a wasted shot. When you hit a bad shot, take a moment to figure out what you did wrong. Put that in your memory bank and "mini-book" and the next time you have that shot, don't do what you did before. Instead, make the needed adjustments. That way, the bad shot becomes a good shot because you just used it as a learning tool. What a novel idea!

When you first start out, you may not have a clue as to why you hit a bad shot, and that is okay. Just continue studying, practicing, and playing, and after a while it will come to you. Until that time, just have fun. To help speed up your learning curve, you may want to check out Chapter 5: Ball Flight Laws and Chapter 20: Faults and Fixes.

Some more thoughts to help you develop a great golf mindset:

- In golf, there are no pictures on the scorecard. It's how many that counts, not how. In other words, we don't care how you get it there—just get it there. (Thanks, DM!)
- In golf, it is more important to have an effective swing than a pretty swing.
- In golf, it is not how far you can hit the ball—it is how consistently you can hit it the needed distance.
- When playing golf, whether you are ahead or behind, you can only make one shot at a time—so ensure that your total focus is on the shot that you are about to make. No matter how good, or not-so-good, your previous shot was, that was your previous shot. To hit a good shot now, your entire focus needs to be on this shot.
- The secret to staying calm and playing consistently great golf is realizing the importance of each shot; they all have equal value. Each shot costs you a stroke. That two-foot putt you are about to make is just as important as that 250-yard drive. Not everyone can hit a 250-yard drive, but everyone can sink a two-foot putt, especially if they study, practice, and play. In golf, as in life, control what you can!
- If you master your short game (putting, chipping, and pitching), you can compete with anyone. And the good thing is that anyone can master their short game, if they study, practice, and play. (There seems to be a theme here, eh?)
- Another good thing about practicing the short game is that it doesn't cost you a cent; you can visit any public golf course and practice your putting, chipping, and pitching all day long, free of charge, when you bring your own clubs and golf balls. I am talking about enjoying the great outdoors, getting full-body exercise, and fantastically improving your golf game—all at the same time. What a sweet deal. Additionally, you may even meet the love of your life since he or she may be out practicing their short game as well. This sweet deal may have just gotten even sweeter. (You are welcome. Please keep those cards and letters coming!)

3
<u>CHAPTER</u>

GRIP

Next to your mindset, your grip is the most important thing in golf because your grip is the only connection you have between yourself and the club. A good golf swing starts with a good grip.

GRIPPING THE CLUB WITH THE LEAD HAND

To get the correct grip on your club, and to grip it at the correct height, start by standing upright with your arms hanging naturally by your sides and your golf club leaning against the outside of your lead leg. For right-handed golfers, your lead leg is your left leg. While the club is leaning against your lead leg, grip the club with your lead hand (left hand for right-handed golfers). Your lead hand is also your glove hand.

When you grip the golf club with your lead hand, your lead thumb should extend down the shaft. The longer your thumb is down the shaft, the longer you should be able to hit the ball.

When gripping the club in your lead hand, the club shaft should run across the base of your last three fingers and through the middle of your index finger. You want to grip the club in your fingers and not your palm. Gripping the club in your fingers allows for more wrist hinge. More wrist hinge equals more power and distance.

GRIP OPTIONS FOR THE TRAIL HAND

After you have properly placed your lead hand on the club, you want to place your trail hand on the club. For right-handed golfers, your trail hand is your right hand.

When it comes to gripping the club with both hands, there are three distinct variations. There is the Vardon grip (overlap grip), the interlock grip, and the ten-finger (baseball) grip.

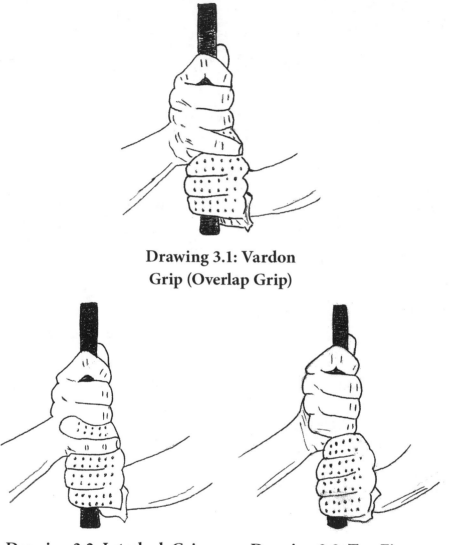

**Drawing 3.1: Vardon
Grip (Overlap Grip)**

Drawing 3.2: Interlock Grip   **Drawing 3.3: Ten-Finger
(Baseball) Grip**

Specifics regarding each grip:

- Vardon Grip (Overlap Grip): Type of grip where the little finger of the right hand lies over the index finger of the left hand (for right-handed golfers). This is a good grip to use if you need more distance because it frees up your wrists for more hinge and power on the downswing.

- Interlock Grip: Type of grip where the little finger of the right hand is entwined with the index finger of the left (for right-handed golfers). This is a good grip to use if you need more accuracy because it firms up your wrists.
- Ten-Finger (Baseball) Grip: Type of grip where you hold the club with all ten fingers. This grip is sometimes used by individuals with small hands. This is a good grip to use if you need more height in your shots because it makes your trail hand the strong hand, which gives you a more sweeping arc and more loft at impact.

Experiment with each of these grips to see which one works best for you. When it comes to these three grips there is no right or wrong choice. The Vardon grip (overlap) is the most popular grip on the PGA Tour (Men's Tour) and the ten-finger (baseball) grip is seldom used. The interlock grip is the most popular on the LPGA Tour (Ladies Tour).

Interesting Fact: The interlock grip, which is the most popular grip on the Ladies Tour, is also the grip used by both Jack Nicklaus and Tiger Woods, two of the greatest male golfers of all time. Knowing this fact, I would say that the interlock grip is probably a grip worth checking out. Again, experiment with each of these grips and then choose the one that works best for you.

GRIP FIRMNESS (OR THE LACK THEREOF)

Grip your club lightly enough that you can feel the weight of the clubhead. Feeling the weight of the clubhead will put the speed of your swing in the clubhead and not the grip end. (If you cannot feel the weight of your clubhead at address and during your swing, you are gripping the club too tightly.)

GRIP STRENGTH

Getting your grip strength correct is vital to the success of your golf game because your grip strength (strong, neutral, or weak) is what determines your clubface direction. Your clubface direction, along with your swing path, is what determines your ball flight.

Your clubface direction determines up to 85% of your ball flight because it determines the initial direction of your ball and the spin you have on it. The remaining 15% of your ball flight is controlled by your swing path. Your swing path is what puts the curvature on the ball. Your swing path is greatly influenced by your setup. Your grip strength and your setup are inseparable. (I will discuss setup in great detail in Chapter 4: Setup.)

Before I discuss the specifics of each grip strength (strong, neutral, or weak), please notice the fleshy part of your hands between your thumb and index finger. You will see a V shape on each hand. The direction that these V's are pointing at address, along with how many knuckles you can see, are what indicates how strong a grip you are using.

Also, before I discuss the specifics of each grip strength, please know that no matter which grip strength you end up going with, after doing the two drills below, ensure that the V's on both hands point in the same direction; otherwise, your hands will be working against each other. In addition, when you grip the club, ensure that your hands are together and not apart.

Specifics of each grip strength:

- Strong Grip: A strong grip has several benefits. It closes the clubface at impact and it helps players draw the ball. In a strong grip, the V's of both hands point up at your trail shoulder and you can see knuckles on your lead hand (left hand for right-handed golfers). The more knuckles you can see on your lead hand, the stronger the grip.
- Neutral Grip: While the strong grip is very popular, some golfers believe that the neutral grip gives you the best chance of hitting the ball straight, because when the palms of both hands are square to the target line at address, they tend to return to a square position at impact. In this grip, the V's on both hands point up at your trail ear and you can see three knuckles on each hand.
- Weak Grip: In the weak grip, the palms are tilted to the left (for right-handed golfers) and the V's of both hands point up at your chin. You can see knuckles on your trail hand. A weak grip produces a natural fade.

To determine the correct grip strength (strong, neutral, or weak) for you, do the following drill. When doing this drill, please know that the correct grip strength for you may be different than the correct grip strength for your playing companions. The correct grip strength for you is the grip that delivers your clubface square to your swing path at impact.

To determine how strong a grip you need to use:

- Hit a handful of shots with your driver. Be sure to use your driver because by using a club with very little loft, such as your driver, if you are hitting the ball with a crossing blow—outside-in or inside-out—you will get a lot of sidespin on the ball.
- If your shots bend from left to right (for right-handed golfers), your clubface is open to your swing path at impact. To eliminate this, take a stronger grip by rotating your left hand on the grip more to the right (for right-handed golfers). Rotate your left (lead) hand just a little bit at a time until you are consistently hitting straight shots, no matter whether these straight shots are going straight

right, straight left, or straight down the middle of your target line. In this part of the drill, your goal is to hit straight shots. When you consistently hit straight shots, no matter where these straight shots go, it means that your clubface direction and your swing path have matched. Congratulations!

- If your shots bend from right to left (for right-handed golfers), the clubface is closed to your swing path at impact. To eliminate this, take a weaker grip by rotating your left hand on the grip more to the left (for right-handed golfers). Rotate your left (lead) hand just a little bit at a time until you are consistently hitting straight shots. Remember, your goal here is to hit straight shots, no matter where these straight shots go. Again, congratulations!

- Once you start consistently hitting straight shots, you will know that your clubface direction and your swing path have matched. If these straight shots are consistently going straight right or straight left, instead of straight down your target line, you will know that your setup is the culprit, because as I mentioned earlier, your setup greatly influences your swing path. To get these straight shots to go straight down your target line, simply adjust your setup. To learn how to adjust your setup, see Chapter 4: Setup.

Now that you know which way your clubface is pointing at impact, do the following drill to clearly learn your swing path:

- Hit a handful of shots with your 9-iron. Because of the loft on your 9-iron, the club contacts the bottom back of the ball, imparting backspin. This backspin overrides the sidespin—therefore, you get a truer picture of your swing path.

- With the lofted club, you are more likely to hit a straight shot because the backspin overrides the sidespin. If you slice the ball with your driver, your lofted club will hit the ball straight left (for right-handed golfers), indicating that you are swinging outside-in. If you are a left-handed golfer and you slice the ball with your driver, you will hit the ball straight right with a lofted club, indicating that you are swinging outside-in.

- If this is indeed what your shots are doing when using your 9-iron, if you are a right-handed golfer and your shots are going straight left, all you have to do is move your aim and stance to the right so that your shots go straight down your target line. If you are a left-handed golfer and your shots are going straight right, all you have to do is move your aim and stance to the left so that your shots go straight down your target line.

To hit straight shots, your clubface direction and your swing path must match. To hit these straight shots straight down your target line, your clubface direction, your swing path, and your target line—all three—must match.

4
CHAPTER

SETUP

A<small>FTER MINDSET AND GRIP, SETUP IS THE NEXT MOST IMPORTANT THING IN GOLF</small> because your setup greatly influences your swing path since you will always swing along your shoulder line. As stated under "Grip Strength" in Chapter 3: Grip, your grip strength and your setup are inseparable. (Please see "Grip Strength" in Chapter 3: Grip, if you haven't already done so.)

When I am speaking about setup, I am speaking about:

- Aim
- Alignment
- Ball Position
- Stance-Width
- Posture
- Weight Distribution
- Trail Leg
- Head, Chin, and Eyes
- Shoulders, Arms, and Hands
- Shaft Lean

AIM

To hit the ball in the right direction, you must first be able to select a target line. To select the correct target line, walk behind your ball five to ten feet or so. Select your target line from there. Do this before all of your shots, including putting, chipping, and pitching.

When selecting a target line, visualize a set of railroad tracks. The ball, clubhead, and target are on the outside rail. For a straight shot straight down your target line, your shoulders, hips, knees, and feet are on the inside rail, parallel to the target line. Of these four (shoulders, hips, knees, and feet) the shoulders are the most important because you will always swing along your shoulder line. For how to set up when you want to hit a fade or a draw, see Chapter 12: Hitting Specialty Shots.

For a straight shot straight down your target line, your target line should be from six to twelve on an imaginary analog clockface lying on the ground, which is lying on top of the outside rail of a set of imaginary railroad tracks. Your shoulders, hips, knees, and feet should be on the inside rail, parallel to the target line. Your swing should be over the outside rail. On the downswing, swing down from the inside, in-to-square-to-in. See Drawing 8.8.

ALIGNMENT

Getting your alignment right is of great importance. If you don't get your alignment right, you can have the most beautiful golf swing in the world—yet you will forever struggle with your golf game. To get your alignment right, approach your ball from behind and not the side, keeping your eyes on the target line you have selected.

For straight shots straight down your target line, when you set up, set the clubface up square to the ball and target line and then set up to the clubface. If you set your body up first and then set the clubface up to the ball, you will forever struggle.

For straight shots straight down your target line, when aiming the clubface, the leading edge must be square to the ball and target line and then your shoulders must be at a right angle (ninety degrees) to that. If your shoulders are not at a right angle (ninety degrees) to the leading edge of your club at address and impact, the ball will be sent offline.

If your club has a closed clubface by design, still set the clubface up square to the ball and target line, and then set your shoulders at a right angle (ninety degrees) to that, adjusting your grip strength (strong, neutral, or weak) to make this happen if need be.

When aiming the clubface at the target:

- Let the club sit on its sole at its natural lie. With the irons, there should be a slight gap between the toe of the club and the ground. Hinge your wrists just enough to allow this to happen.
- When lining up the clubface with the ball, have the ball in line with the toe of the club when the clubhead is lying on the ground. You do this so that when you raise the club up off the ground to start the backswing, the ball will be in the heart of the club.

When you set up to the clubface, it may feel as if your shoulders are aiming left of the target (for right-handed golfers) because you are standing to the side of your ball. Your ball should be in line with your target because you strike the ball with your clubface and not your body.

To ensure that your setup is correct, when you are practicing, place a club or an alignment stick on the ground just outside your golf ball. Place another club or alignment stick in front of your toes parallel to the first club or alignment stick. Now take a club and hold it across your knees and then across your chest. The club that you hold across your knees and then your chest should run exactly parallel to the club that runs along your feet.

When it comes to aim and alignment, there are two very distinct methods. With both methods, you walk five to ten feet or so behind your ball to determine your target line.

With the first method, "Aiming Straight at the Target," select an intermediate target that is in line with your true target. Aim your clubface square to your ball and the intermediate target with the idea that it is a lot easier to aim and align with a nearby object than some target in the distance. The intermediate target you choose should be something just a foot or two in front of your ball, target side.

With the second method, "Visualizing a Set of Goalposts," step behind the ball to select the target line and then take into consideration your natural ball flight. Rather than aiming at an intermediate target, visualize a set of goalposts. Aim and align for your ball to end up in the center of the goalposts, allowing for your natural ball flight.

To determine your natural ball flight, remember what your first five or six shots did when you were doing the first drill under "Grip Strength" in Chapter 3: Grip. If you haven't done that drill, or you can't recall what your first five or six shots did, do the drill the first chance you get. This drill can forever change your game and possibly your life.

When doing the drill:

- Hit a handful of shots with your driver. Be sure to use your driver because by using a club with very little loft, such as your driver, if you are hitting the ball with a crossing blow—outside-in or inside-out—you will get a lot of sidespin on the ball.
- If you are a right-handed golfer and your first five or six shots start out left and then curve back to the right, you hit a natural fade. To play your natural fade, rather than aiming straight at the target, aim a little left and let the ball curve back to the target.
- If you are a right-handed golfer and your first five or six shots start out right and then curve back to the left, you hit a natural draw. To play your natural draw, rather than aiming straight at the target, aim a little right and let the ball curve back to the target.

Both of the methods for aiming and aligning work extremely well. Try them both and then adopt the one that works better for you.

BALL POSITION

Correct ball position encourages correct aim and alignment. To play the ball in the correct position in your stance, there are two distinct schools of thought. Both of these methods work extremely well. Why not try them both and then adopt the one that works better for you?

With the first school of thought, the position of the ball in your stance will vary according to the length of the club as follows:

- With your driver, play the ball forward in your stance. The ball position should be in line with your lead heel.
- With a wedge, play the ball in the center of your stance.
- With all other clubs, the ball would be played somewhere between those two parameters: the longer the club, the more forward the ball.

The second school of thought is to keep the ball in the same position with all of your clubs for full standard shots:

- With your driver, play the ball in line with your shirt logo and take a wide stance. This would allow you to hit the ball with an ascending blow because the ball will be teed up and will be ahead of the bottom of your swing (which is under your chin). With your driver, you want to hit the ball on the upswing.

- With a middle iron, play the ball in the same place in your stance—but take a narrower stance. This will put you more on top of the ball and allow you to swing down on the ball, taking a slight divot on the target side of the ball.
- With short irons and wedges, play the ball in the same place but have the narrowest stance. This allows you to hit down on the ball at a steeper angle, taking a fairly good-sized divot on the target side of the ball.

No matter which of these two methods you go with, to ensure that you are set up the correct distance from the ball at address, do the following:

- Set up to the ball with the club at its natural lie and with your arms relaxed and hanging straight down from your shoulder sockets.
- Remove your trail arm from the club. (For right-handed golfers, the trail arm is your right arm.) The trail arm should hang down naturally right beside the lead arm. If not, your arms are not hanging straight down and relaxed from your shoulder sockets.

STANCE-WIDTH

No matter where you play your ball in your stance, ensure that you have the correct stance-width for the club you are using and for the shot you are about to make. If your stance is too wide, it will be hard to turn on your backswing. If your stance is too narrow, you will lose your balance during the downswing, making good ball striking difficult.

Note: If you are somewhat consistently losing your balance during your swing, either your stance is too narrow or you are overswinging. Pay attention to both your stance-width and your swing effort to determine which one is the culprit and then make the needed correction.

When it comes to stance-width, the longer your club, the wider your stance should be. The shorter the club, the narrower your stance should be. For the middle irons (5-, 6-, 7-iron), the insides of your feet should be shoulder-width apart. For the woods/metals and long irons, the insides of your feet should be two inches wider. For the short irons and wedges, the insides of your feet should be two inches narrower.

No matter which club you are using, play the ball forward enough in your stance and have a wide enough stance that you never feel as if you have to sway on your backswing to get behind the ball. If you sway on your backswing instead of turn, there is no way that you can consistently come back to the same spot in your downswing. Consistently coming back to the same spot in your downswing is what allows you to consistently make great golf shots.

POSTURE

To make consistent golf shots you must have good posture. Good posture is what allows you to make a good turn on the backswing, downswing, and follow-through. If you don't have good posture, your swing will be very inconsistent. If your swing is inconsistent, your shots will be inconsistent too. For an example of good posture, see Drawing 8.1.

When it comes to posture, you should have the same body lean with every club. The only difference is that with the shorter clubs, you will have more knee flex. However, if you are of short stature, don't flex your knees too much because you want to swing on a wide arc. The taller you stand, the wider your swing arc will be. The wider your swing arc, the more distance and power you will get.

When you are in the correct posture, your chest should be facing the ground and your arms should be hanging straight down from your shoulder sockets. If your chest is down, the club will be down. From address to impact, the distance between the center of your chest and the ball should remain the same. To make this happen, you must maintain the same spine angle. To maintain the same spine angle, keep the same flex in your trail leg from address through impact and visualize you have a rod driven through the top of your head and straight down your spine. Swing around your spine because the spine is the axis of the swing. I repeat, the spine is the axis of the swing.

To set up in good posture:

- Stand upright with your club resting against your side.
- Flex your knees and bend forward from your hips and not your waist. When you lean forward from your hips, your buttocks will protrude behind you. Your buttocks protruding behind you will counterbalance your weight over your feet.
- When bending forward, allow your arms to hang freely beneath your shoulder sockets. Stop bending forward when your hands hang over your toe line. At address, you should be looking in at your hands and not out at them. If you are looking out at them, you are reaching for the ball.
- When your arms are hanging straight down and relaxed beneath your shoulder sockets, and your hands hang over your toe line, grab your club from your side and sole it on the ground. You are now in perfect posture!

WEIGHT DISTRIBUTION

Set up with your weight correctly divided between your feet depending on the club you are using and the shot you are making. See the following:

<u>Weight Distribution at Address</u>

Woods/Metals (including driver)	40/60 (lead foot/trail foot)
Long Irons	50/50 (lead foot/trail foot)
Middle Irons (5-, 6-, 7-iron)	60/40 (lead foot/trail foot)
Short Irons (8-, 9-iron, wedges)	60/40 (lead foot/trail foot)

Set up with your weight distributed evenly over your feet, front and back, toes to heels. If you have your weight too much on your heels, you will raise up during your backswing and will probably hit the ball thin on the downswing. If you have your weight too far forward on your toes, you will lose your balance on the downswing and there is no telling where your ball will go.

TRAIL LEG

When you set up to your clubface, you want to have a little flex in your trail leg and you want to maintain this flex from address through impact. If you straighten your trail leg on the backswing or any time before impact, you will change your swing plane, which will make it difficult to consistently come back to the same spot at impact.

On the downswing, you want to have the feeling that you are hitting your lead knee with your trail knee. This will have you getting your weight to the lead side on the downswing. If you don't get your weight to the lead side on the downswing and follow-through, all the golf pointers in the world won't help you. (Thanks, SH!)

To get your weight to the lead side on the downswing, visualize there is a ball two to five inches in front of your ball on the target side. Swing down as if that were the ball you were hitting.

HEAD, CHIN, AND EYES

At address, your head should be at the same angle as your spine, with your chin up. Having your chin up, out of your chest, allows you to turn your lead shoulder under your chin on the backswing and turn your trail shoulder under your chin on the downswing. On the backswing, your lead shoulder goes under your chin while your trail shoulder goes up. This is what makes it a golf swing and not a baseball swing.

The lowest point in your swing will always be where your weight is, which is under your head. With the long clubs, you want your head to be behind the ball at impact because you want to sweep the ball off the turf or tee. Keeping your head behind the ball with the long clubs until after impact will allow you to sweep the ball off the turf or tee and will help increase clubhead speed at impact. With the short irons and wedges, you want your head to be over the ball at impact. Having your head over the ball with the short irons and wedges is what allows you to hit down on the ball.

Keep your eyes focused on the ball from address through impact. With the long clubs, keep your eyes focused on the back of the ball. With the short irons and wedges, keep your eyes focused on the front of the ball. For a draw, keep your eyes focused on the back inside quadrant of the ball.

SHOULDERS, ARMS, AND HANDS

At address, your arms should hang straight down and relaxed from your shoulder sockets. Your hands should hang over your toe line.

At address, your hands should hang in a slot located just forward of your pants zipper and just off the inside of your lead thigh. If you go with the first school of thought shared under "Ball Position," with the short irons and wedges, the grip end of the club should point at the crease in your front pant leg. With your driver, the grip end of the club should point at your pants zipper. With all other clubs, the grip end of the club should point somewhere between those two parameters.

The ideal hands-to-body distance varies depending on which expert you listen to. Some instructors state that a good rule of thumb is to have the hands a palm's width from the body for short and middle irons and a palm's length for long irons, hybrids, and woods/metals. Other experts say that you should keep the hands the same distance (five inches or so) from the body, no matter the club. I say that you should try both approaches and go with the one that works better for you. In golf, as with most things in life, there are no absolutes—just guidelines!

SHAFT LEAN

If you go with the first school of thought shared under "Ball Position," at address, the shaft of your club will appear to lean slightly toward the target with your short irons and wedges. This is because, with the first school of thought, the ball is played in the center of your stance with the short irons and wedges. With the middle irons, the shaft of the club appears to lean less toward the target since the ball is forward of center. With long irons, hybrids, and woods/metals, the shaft of the club appears to be in line. This is because while the ball position moves forward, the hands stay in the same place (in a slot located just forward of your pants zipper and just off the inside of your lead thigh). With your driver, the shaft leans away from the target because the ball is played the farthest forward in your stance, in line with your lead heel. With your driver, the shaft leans toward your pants zipper at address.

5
<u>CHAPTER</u>

BALL FLIGHT LAWS

AFTER MINDSET, GRIP, AND SETUP, UNDERSTANDING BALL FLIGHT LAWS MAY BE THE next most important thing in golf. If you don't know why your ball goes where it goes, it will be hard to get it to go where you want it to go consistently. If you don't know why your ball goes where it goes, it will be hard to change where it goes if it needs to be changed.

As stated under "Grip Strength" in Chapter 3: Grip, your ball flight is determined by your clubface direction (85%) and by your swing path (15%). Your clubface direction is determined by your grip strength (strong, neutral, or weak) and your swing path is greatly influenced by your setup because you will always swing along your shoulder line. Your grip strength and your setup are inseparable. (If you don't have a full understanding of this concept, please revisit the two drills under "Grip Strength" in Chapter 3: Grip.)

Your ball flight is determined so much (85 percent) by the direction and angle that your clubface is pointing at impact because your clubface direction at impact determines the initial direction of your ball and the spin you have on it. Spin creates the sideways movement of your shot. This spin affects the movement of your golf ball while it is in the air and after it hits the ground. In other words, if your ball is spinning to the right in the air, it will probably continue spinning right once it lands. That is why you can hit a shot that lands in the middle of the fairway yet have it end up in trouble before it stops rolling.

If you have an open clubface at impact (clubface pointing to the right of your swing path for right-handed golfers), the ball will generally have a clockwise spin on it. If the clubface is closed at impact (clubface pointing to the left of your swing path for right-handed golfers), you will get a counterclockwise spin on it.

For a better understanding of the ball flight laws, see the "Ball Flight Laws Diagram" that follows. This diagram is from a right-handed golfer's perspective. The diagram shows the nine possible ball flights and offers an abbreviated explanation for what causes them. More detailed explanations follow the diagram. When viewing the diagram, please check out the abbreviated explanations as well as the detailed explanations.

When studying the "Ball Flight Laws Diagram," you will be able to note just how much of the ball flight is truly determined by the direction that your clubface is pointing at impact. For example, Ball Flights #1, #2, and #3 are all a result of a swing path pretty much straight down the target line. The difference in the ball flights is caused solely by the difference in the clubface direction at impact. Please note that where the ball ends up varies greatly just because of the difference in the clubface direction at impact.

Ball Flights #4, #5, and #6 are all caused by an out-to-in swing (for right-handed golfers). The difference in the ball flights is caused by the difference in the clubface direction at impact. Ball Flights #7, #8, and #9 are all caused by an in-to-out swing (for right-handed golfers). Again, the difference in the ball flights is caused by the difference in the clubface direction at impact.

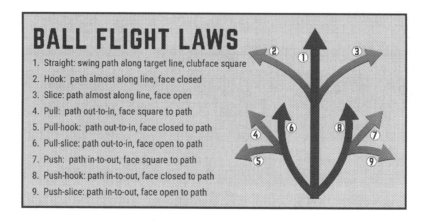

Ball Flight #1: Straight Shot Straight Down Your Target Line - This is for both right-handed and left-handed golfers. With a straight shot straight down your target line, the ball starts straight and flies straight along the target line because your swing path and clubface are both square to the target line at impact. Your swing is actually from in-to-square-to-in; your clubface will be square to the target line for just a fraction of a second. This is a very desirable shot! See Chapter 12: Hitting Specialty Shots for additional pointers on how to hit straight shots straight down your target line.

Ball Flight #2: Hook - This is for right-handed golfers. With a hook, the ball starts a little right of the target and then bends to the left. The clubhead is traveling slightly across your target line from in-to-out during impact with a closed clubface (the face is facing left of the target line). This creates counterclockwise sidespin that bends the ball left once it starts to slow down.

Ball Flight #3: Slice - This is for right-handed golfers. With a slice, the ball starts a little left of the target and then bends to the right. The clubhead is traveling slightly across your target line from out-to-in during impact, with the clubface open (facing right of your target line). This creates a clockwise sidespin that bends the ball to the right once it starts to slow down. The more the clubface is open, the more the slice and usually the weaker the shot because you will be striking the ball higher up and hitting it with more of a glancing blow.

Ball Flight #4: Pull - This is for right-handed golfers. With a pull, the ball flies in a straight line but to the left of the target. The clubhead is traveling across your target line from out-to-in during impact. The clubface is square to your swing path but not to your target line. These shots are usually struck well because the clubface and the swing path matched at impact. The only problem is that the shot is going left instead of toward the target.

Ball Flight #5: Pull-Hook - This is for right-handed golfers. With a pull-hook, the ball starts left of the target and then bends farther to the left. The clubhead is traveling across your target line from out-to-in, but this time the clubface is closed to your swing path. This combination of two faults in the same direction sends the ball far left.

Ball Flight #6: Pull-Slice - This is for right-handed golfers. With a pull-slice, the ball starts left of the target and then bends to the right. The clubhead is traveling across your target line from out-to-in with the clubface open. If you can control the amount of slice on this shot, it is a very desirable shot and is referred to as a fade. See Chapter 12: Hitting Specialty Shots for additional pointers on how to hit a fade.

Ball Flight #7: Push - This is for right-handed golfers. With a push, the ball flies straight but to the right of the target. The clubhead is traveling across your target line at impact, but this time from in-to-out. The clubface is square to your swing path but not to your target line. The shot will feel powerful but it is offline.

Ball Flight #8: Push-Hook - This is for right-handed golfers. With a push-hook, the ball starts right of your target and then bends to the left. The clubhead is traveling across your target line at impact from in-to-out with the clubface closed. If you can control the amount of hook on this shot, it is a very desirable shot and is referred to as a draw. See Chapter 12: Hitting Specialty Shots for additional pointers on how to hit a draw.

Ball Flight #9: Push-Slice - This is for right-handed golfers. With a push-slice, the ball starts right of your target and then bends more to the right. The clubhead is traveling across your target line from in-to-out at impact, but this time the clubface is open to your swing path. These two faults combining in the same direction send the ball far right.

When you go to the driving range, take the "Ball Flight Laws Diagram" with you—along with the detailed explanations. This will allow you to analyze every shot you hit. If the ball went where you wanted it to go, ensure that you know why so you can repeat it. If the ball didn't go where you wanted it to go, determine why.

Of the nine possible ball flights represented on the "Ball Flight Laws Diagram," there are three that you want to master—the straight shot, the fade, and the draw:

- The straight shot: For the straight shot, see Ball Flight #1. This is for both right-handed and left-handed golfers.
- The fade: If you are a right-handed golfer, see Ball Flight #6. If you are a left-handed golfer, see Ball Flight #8 but read abbreviated explanation #6.
- The draw: If you are a right-handed golfer, see Ball Flight #8. If you are a left-handed golfer, see Ball Flight #6 but read abbreviated explanation #8.

The straight shot, the fade, and the draw are the nucleus of your golf game. By all means, take the time to study, practice, and then play them. For detailed pointers on how to hit these three shots, see Chapter 12: Hitting Specialty Shots.

Note: When a right-handed golfer needs to hit a fade, a left-handed golfer needs to hit a draw. When a right-handed golfer needs to hit a draw, a left-handed golfer needs to hit a fade.

6
CHAPTER

THE GOLF SWING

IT HAS BEEN SAID THAT THE GOLF SWING CAN BE AS SIMPLE AS CHECKERS OR AS complicated as chess. If that is true, then I guess this chapter is the checkers part and Chapter 7: The Golf Swing (Broken Down) is the chess part. Please read through both of these chapters and jot down any pointers that really jump out at you. When doing this, please remember that every golfer is looking for the same thing—that one pointer that will put their game over the top. I found mine. (Thanks, SC!) I hope you find yours!

According to Wikipedia ("golf swing"),[1] the goal of the golf swing is to direct as much kinetic energy as possible into the clubhead so that when it comes into contact with the ball, all of the energy will transfer to the ball, sending it into flight. Wikipedia states that this entire process, the golf swing, starts with the stance. Wikipedia states that it is critical to make sure that the golfer has a low center of gravity so that he or she can remain balanced throughout the swing.

Wikipedia goes on to state that the swing starts with the arms moving back in a straight line. When the clubhead reaches the level of the hip, two things happen: there is a stern wrist cock that acts as a hinge, along with the lead knee (left knee for right-handed golfers) building up its torque by moving into the same line as the belly button before the start of the upswing. As the swing continues to the top of the backswing, the golfer's lead arm (left arm for right-handed golfers) should be fully extended and the trail arm should be hinged at the elbow.

According to Wikipedia, the downswing begins with the hips and the lower body rather than the arms and upper body, with emphasis on the wrist cock. As the golfer's

---

[1] Wikipedia contributors, "Golf swing," *Wikipedia, The Free Encyclopedia*, https://en.wikipedia.org/w/index.php?title=Golf_swing&oldid=1030401500 [accessed June 30, 2021]

hips turn into the shot, the trail elbow drops straight down, hugging the trail side of the golfer's torso. As the trail elbow drops, the wrists begin to snap through from the wrist cock in the backswing. A solid extension of the arms and good transfer of body weight on the downswing and follow-through should put the golfer leaning up on his or her trail big toe, balanced, with the golf club resting on the back of the golfer's neck.

Wikipedia goes on to state that it is important that all of the movements occur with precise timing, while the head remains completely still with the eyes focused on the ball throughout the entire swing. I believe most golf experts would agree with Wikipedia's description of the golf swing, other than the head remaining completely still, and the lower body beginning the downswing when you are using a short iron or wedge. With the short irons and wedges, the clubhead initiates the downswing. When using a short iron or wedge, if you start the downswing with your lower body (knees and hips), you will swing outside-in and will most likely pull the ball.

Another way of looking at the golf swing is that it is a push-pull motion. You push the club on the backswing and you pull on the downswing. Unfortunately, according to the golf experts, most amateurs do the opposite. They pull on the backswing and push on the downswing. If you push on the downswing, your trail arm and trail hand will take over and your swing will be very erratic. If your swing is erratic, your shots will be erratic too.

On the downswing, pull the grip end of your club down with your lead arm as if you were jamming the butt of the club against an imaginary wall. Keep pulling the grip end of the club down all the way through the swing until the lead hand reaches hip-high on the follow-through. While pulling the grip end of the club down and through, turn your belt buckle toward the target. This will have you getting your weight to the lead side on the downswing and follow-through, have you getting your hands to the ball before the clubhead, and have you hitting the ball farther than you ever have. (Thanks, SC!)

When you are pulling the grip end of your club down and through (previous thought), know that when the clubhead is going down, your hands are actually going up. This is what keeps you from bottoming out and is what puts the speed of your swing in the clubhead and not the grip end. These two moves combined will have you hitting shots off the chart. (Thanks, RTG!)

Another key thing to know about the golf swing is that it is an up-and-down swing and not an around swing. This is what makes it a golf swing and not a baseball swing.

On the backswing, take the club back and then up. On the downswing, take the club down and then forward. On the downswing, if you take the club down toward the ball instead of down and then forward, you will probably hit the shot thin. To help you with this pointer regarding the downswing, remember what Wikipedia says about the downswing. Wikipedia states, "As the golfer's hips turn into the shot, the trail elbow drops straight down, hugging the trail side of the golfer's torso."

An additional way to look at the golf swing is that it is a lot like slinging a ten-pound bag of potatoes. (Thanks, GS!) You sling the bag back and then you sling the bag forward. If you visualize and/or attempt to sling a ten-pound bag of something, you will come to realize that even though you are attempting to sling the bag straight back, your shoulders will eventually sling the bag back on the inside and then sling it down and through from the inside.

On the downswing, you would never be able to sling the ten-pound bag of potatoes down outside-in—and you would not want to. On the downswing with a golf club, you would never want to swing down from outside-in unless you were trying to hit a fade or were in a greenside bunker. (To learn how to hit a fade, see Chapter 12: Hitting Specialty Shots; to learn how to hit from greenside bunkers, see Chapter 15: Hitting from Greenside Bunkers.)

When swinging your driver, instead of visualizing you are slinging a ten-pound bag of potatoes, visualize slinging a bale of hay onto a low trailer. This will have you heavy on your feet and will have you using the same motion as slinging the ten-pound bag. When slinging a bale of hay, there is no way that you could sling it outside-in and you never would want to. When visualizing slinging a bale of hay onto a low trailer, you would actually be swinging up toward the end of your sling/swing. When swinging your driver, you want to be swinging up at impact because your ball will be played forward in your stance and it will be teed up. With driver, you want to hit the ball with an ascending blow.

If you hit down on the ball with your driver, you will probably lose a lot of distance (twenty to thirty yards). With your driver, if you don't play your ball far enough forward in your stance, you may have your hands ahead of the ball at address and impact. If you have your hands ahead of the ball at impact, you will indeed be hitting down on the ball because having your hands ahead of the ball delofts the club. With your driver, your ball should be played in line with your lead heel and the grip end of your club should point toward your pants zipper at address. With your driver, at impact, your hands and clubhead get to the ball at the same time—not your hands before the ball.

Another great visual regarding the golf swing is that on full shots, the club should point toward the target five different times during the swing:

- The first time is when you are halfway back on your backswing, in the nine o'clock position. In the nine o'clock position, the grip end of the club should point toward the target.
- The second time is when you are at the top of the swing. At the top of the swing, the clubhead should point toward the target.
- The third time is when you are halfway down on the downswing, in the nine o'clock position. In the nine o'clock position, again, the grip end of the club should point toward the target.
- The fourth time is when you are halfway through on the follow-through, in the three o'clock position. In the three o'clock position, the clubhead should point toward the target.
- The fifth time is when you are in the finish position. In the finish position, the grip end of the club should point toward the target.

To understand the nine o'clock and three o'clock positions, think of having your back to an analog clockface with twelve o'clock above your head, nine o'clock to your right (for right-handed golfers), six o'clock at your feet, and three o'clock to your left (for right-handed golfers). For a clearer understanding of this, see Drawing 8.9.

In the golf swing there are two chief movements: the sledgehammer and the scythe movement. If you put these two together, you will have an awesome golf swing with unbelievable clubhead speed. In the sledgehammer movement, the wrists and the arms together create and up-and-down movement similar to swinging a sledgehammer. In the scythe movement, the body turn and weight shift combine to make a movement similar to an individual cutting grass with an old-fashioned scythe. The up-and-down movement (sledgehammer) happens halfway back on your backswing and halfway down on your downswing. The up-and-down movement is straight up and down along your target line and not at an angle. Take the club back—and then up. Take the club down—and then forward. To master these two movements:

- Practice the two movements using a 7-iron without a ball present.
- Practice the two movements using a 7-iron, hitting balls making half-swings.
- Practice the two movements using a 7-iron, hitting balls making full swings.
- Practice the two movements hitting full shots with all of your clubs.

When it comes to the golf swing, you want to develop a great swing and just let the ball get in the way. To get the feeling for this, practice swinging without a ball. Swinging without a ball takes away the tension of worrying about where the ball is going to go and replaces it with good tempo and rhythm. When doing this drill, use your 7-iron. Brush the ground on the backswing and then brush the ground on the downswing.

Another great drill to help you with your swing is to hit balls with your feet together. Hitting balls with your feet together will keep you from overswinging and will let you clearly see what your arms are supposed to do during the swing. When doing this drill, use your driver and place the ball on a low tee.

Before getting to breaking the golf swing down, which I will do in the next chapter, I would like to cover a few more topics related to the golf swing. The better you understand these topics, the better your golf swing and golf game will be.

SWING PLANE

You should always swing on plane. To swing on plane, visualize swinging along a slanted tabletop, with the tabletop slanted at the same angle as your club shaft at address. With the long clubs, your swing plane will be more horizontal. With the short irons and wedges, your swing plane will be more vertical. Folding your trail arm at the elbow on the backswing while hinging your wrists and folding your lead arm at the elbow on the follow-through while rehinging your wrists, allows you to swing on plane.

Your swing plane affects the angle at which the clubhead hits the ball and dictates the amount and type of spin on the ball. The steeper swing plane of the short irons and wedges creates backspin; the more horizontal plane of the long clubs produces overspin. Backspin decreases the roll, and overspin increases the roll once the ball hits the ground.

It is good to remember these facts about backspin and overspin when you are hitting approach shots. If you are using a short club, you may be able to land the ball on the green and have it stick because of the backspin. If you are using a long club, you may need the ball to land before the green and let the overspin propel it onto the green. See "Approach Shot" in Chapter 12: Hitting Specialty Shots.

SWING PATH

Your swing path will always be along your shoulder line. For this reason, always ensure that you set up correctly to the ball. For right-handed golfers, for a straight shot straight down your target line, set up with your shoulders, hips, knees, and feet parallel to the target line, which is six o'clock to twelve o'clock on an imaginary analog clockface lying on the ground, lying on top of an imaginary outside rail (railroad tracks). See Drawing 8.8.

If you set up parallel to the six o'clock to twelve o'clock line and have your clubface square to the ball and target line, you should hit a straight shot straight down your target line every time from a level lie, excluding the wind factor. From a level lie, the only time your shot would not go exactly straight down your target line is if your clubface is open or closed at impact. If you are not hitting your shots straight down your target line from a level lie, check your clubface direction at address as well as your setup because one of these factors is the culprit.

If you set up with your clubface square to the ball and target line at address but cut across the ball on the downswing, by swinging outside-in or inside-out, your setup is the culprit because your setup greatly influences your swing path. You will always swing along your shoulder line. However, if in an effort to hit the ball farther, you spin out during the downswing, your good setup will probably not be enough to save your shot!

WEIGHT SHIFT

Set up with the proper weight distribution at address as discussed under "Weight Distribution" in Chapter 4: Setup. On the backswing, turn/coil around the inside of your trail leg while shifting your weight to the inside of your trail foot. On the downswing, swing around a stiff lead leg while shifting your weight to the outside of your lead foot.

On the backswing, see if you can turn your trail shoulder to where the center of your back was at address. You can't actually do this but that is the feeling you want to have.

On the backswing, you want to turn/coil and not sway. To help keep you from swaying, imagine having a golf ball under the outside of your trail heel.

On the downswing, get your weight to the lead side. If you don't get your weight to the lead side on the downswing and follow-through, all the golf pointers in the world won't help you. (Thanks, SH!)

To get your weight to the lead side on the downswing, visualize there is a ball two to five inches on the target side of your ball. Swing down as if that were the ball you were hitting.

When it comes to weight shift, the feeling you want is the same feeling you would have if you were throwing a baseball or a football, hitting a forehand shot in tennis, or bowling. In all of these activities, you would shift your weight to the trail side on the backswing and then shift your weight to the lead side on the downswing. To better understand this feeling, take a moment and mimic these motions.

On the downswing, if your weight moves away from the target instead of toward the target, your swing arc will move away from the target as well. If your swing arc moves away from the target on your downswing, your chances of hitting a good golf shot are between slim and none—and slim has already headed for the pro shop.

HANDS IN THE GOLF SWING

When it comes to the hands in the golf swing, there are two distinct schools of thought. I will share them both, while subscribing to the latter. Note: The latter school of thought is the one that Jack Nicklaus, possibly the greatest golfer of all time, subscribes to.

No matter which school of thought you go with, please know that with all clubs, other than your driver and putter, your hands should get to the ball before your clubhead. With your driver and putter, your hands and the clubhead get to the ball at the same time.

In the first school of thought, the lead hand supplies the control and the trail hand supplies the power. In this school of thought, you open, square, and close the clubface with your lead hand, while providing the power with your trail hand much as you do on long putts. In the first school of thought, your lead hand is what controls the clubface, and not your body. On the backswing, the lead hand opens the clubface. On the downswing, the lead hand squares the clubface to the ball and target line. On the follow-through, the lead hand closes the clubface.

The ones who go with this school of thought state that if you slice or hook the ball, it is probably because the wrong hand (your trail hand) is controlling the clubface. They even recommend that to get the feel of controlling the clubface with your lead hand, you should grip a golf club with your lead hand only (left hand for right-handed golfers) and practice opening the clubface on the backswing, squaring the clubface to the imaginary ball and target line at impact, and closing the clubface on the follow-through.

The ones who go with the first school of thought state that the trail hand controls the hinging effect of the hands and therefore the shaft angle at impact. They go on to state that controlling the shaft angle and unhinging the wrists immediately after impact is what provides the power and distance. When using the long clubs, you should visualize driving a nail straight into the back of the ball with your trail hand. When using the short clubs, visualize driving a tent peg into the back of the ball at a 45-degree angle with your trail hand. And when you are attempting to hit a draw, visualize driving a nail or tent peg, depending on which club you are using, into the back-inside quadrant of the ball with your trail hand.

While all of the aforementioned thoughts are great and do indeed lead to power and distance, they also lead to something else—inconsistency. Inconsistency is not what you want in your golf swing.

Another problem I have found when you go with the first school of thought regarding the trail hand providing the power, is that the trail hand has a tendency to take over the swing. That is not a good thing because when the trail hand and/or trail arm takes over the swing, there is no telling where your ball is going to go. It also highly contradicts the pointer shared earlier by the experts stating that you push on the backswing and pull on the downswing.

In the first school of thought, you use your small muscles (arms and hands). In the second school of thought, you use your big muscles—hips, core, and shoulders.

In the second school of thought, you square the clubface with your body—not your hands. Squaring the clubface with your body leads to more consistency in your golf swing because it removes the need for perfect timing. It also removes the fault of flipping your wrists and/or casting your club. Flipping your wrists leads to offline shots. Casting your club leads to weak shots.

Squaring the clubface with your body for accurate shots is easy when your clubface direction at address and your swing path match your target line. To refresh your memory on how to match your clubface direction at address and your swing path to your target line, see "Grip Strength" in Chapter 3: Grip.

To further state the case for going with the second school of thought, check out the following drill for hitting your long irons. When practicing, place a thin towel on the ground an inch behind your ball. Swing down so that you hit the ball and not the towel. The key to hitting the ball and not the towel is not in your hands and arms but in turning your big muscles (shoulders, core, hips) through the target and getting your weight to the lead side. With this motion, your hands just go along for the ride.

Again, this is the school of thought that Jack Nicklaus, possibly the greatest golfer of all time, subscribes to. As with everything else, try both methods and then go with the one that works better for you.

TEMPO AND RHYTHM

When it comes to tempo and rhythm in the golf swing, tempo is the speed at which you swing the club, and rhythm is its fluency. To find your natural tempo and rhythm, concentrate on swinging the golf club smoothly.

When attempting to find your natural tempo and rhythm, start with your sand wedge and start with half swings. Swing back to nine o'clock and then swing down and through to three o'clock. Once you consistently make good, solid strikes, lengthen your swing to three-quarter swings, ten o'clock to two o'clock, and then full swings, eleven thirty to eleven thirty. Once you have completed these steps with your sand wedge, go through the same process with all of your clubs, excluding your putter. Note: When doing this drill, don't attempt to hit to a specified distance. Let the club and your swing determine the correct distance for you for each club.

Please see the following paragraph for an understanding of how to swing back to nine o'clock, ten, eleven thirty, etc. Note: When I am talking about swinging back and through to these different times, I am talking about taking your hands to these times. The club will usually go back and through a little farther. In addition to seeing the following paragraph, see Drawing 8.9.

To get a feel for how far to take your hands back and through on a half swing, a three-quarters swing, and a full swing, think of having your back to an analog clockface with twelve o'clock above your head, nine o'clock to your right (for right-handed golfers), six o'clock at your feet, and three o'clock to your left (for right-handed golfers). On a half swing, swing your hands back to nine o'clock and then through to three o'clock. On a three-quarters swing, swing your hands back to ten o'clock and then through to two o'clock. On a full swing, swing your hands back to eleven thirty and then through to eleven thirty.

The secret to keeping good tempo and rhythm when you are playing is to always use plenty of club. As a rule of thumb, always use more club than you think you need until proven wrong. For example, if you think that a particular shot calls for a 7-iron, use a 6-iron instead. You should be able to hit a 6-iron ten yards farther than a 7-iron. If you consistently start going too long using the 6-iron, then change over to the 7-iron.

If you lose your tempo and rhythm when playing a round of golf, regain it by playing to a shorter target. Reduce the distance you try to hit each club by about one-third. Rather than hitting a 7-iron, you may have to go with a 5-iron. This automatically slows down your swing. By not trying to kill the ball, you will soon regain your tempo and rhythm.

ADDITIONAL THOUGHTS ABOUT THE GOLF SWING

During the swing, at least one arm must be fully extended at all times. From address to the start of your follow-through, your lead arm should be fully extended. Immediately after impact, both arms should be fully extended. From a little after impact to the finish, the trail arm should be fully extended. Keeping at least one arm fully extended is what leads to a repeatable swing.

Don't try to hit the ball harder because when you attempt to hit the ball harder, you tighten your muscles. Tight muscles rob power and distance. Instead of trying to hit the ball harder, hit it farther. To hit the ball farther, take a long club and use a long backswing. In addition, to hit the ball farther, swing all the way through to the finish. If you don't swing through to the finish, you will probably not like where your ball finishes. Also, remember, on full shots, the ball is just the halfway point in your swing.

For short shots, take a short club and a short backswing. Don't take a long backswing and then decelerate on the downswing. If you decelerate on the downswing, you will lose all control of your swing and the ball.

On the downswing, don't try to guide your club because when you try to guide your club instead of swinging your club, your swing gets short and hesitant. A short and hesitant swing usually leads to not-so-good results. Instead of trying to guide your club, trust your grip strength (strong, neutral, or weak), your setup, and your swing.

7
CHAPTER

THE GOLF SWING
(BROKEN DOWN)

EVEN THOUGH IN THIS CHAPTER I AM BREAKING DOWN THE GOLF SWING, PLEASE realize that the golf swing is actually not broken down; it is one smooth, fluid motion. If you were to actually break down the golf swing, you would end up with a choppy swing and choppy results. Instead of breaking down your golf swing, when practicing, merely select a thought or pointer to work on. Focus on that thought or pointer until you get it into your DNA. Once you have that thought or pointer in your DNA, select another one to get into your DNA.

BACKSWING

- The length of your backswing controls your distance. For long shots, take a long club and use a long backswing.
- As stated earlier, the golf swing is a push-pull motion. You push on the backswing.
- As stated earlier, the golf swing is also an up-and-down swing. On the backswing, you swing back and then up.
- On the backswing, turn—do not sway. If you sway on the backswing, there is no way that you can consistently return to the same spot in your downswing.
- On the backswing, turn your shoulders back ninety degrees while turning your hips back forty-five degrees. If you can't turn your shoulders back ninety degrees, turn them as far back as you can without coming up out of your posture.
- To help you turn your shoulders back ninety degrees, go with the thought of trying to turn your trail shoulder to where the center of your back was at address. You will not be able to do this, but that is the feeling you want to have.

- On the backswing, turn your lead shoulder under your chin while your trail shoulder goes up. This is what makes it a golf swing and not a baseball swing.
- On the backswing, use your big muscles (shoulders, core, hips) by keeping your arms connected to your chest. To keep your arms connected to your chest, feel as if you have a glove stuck under your lead arm and you are trying to keep it there for as long as possible during your backswing.
- On the backswing (and throughout the swing), swing around your spine.
- On the backswing, swing on plane. Your swing plane should match your club shaft angle at address. With the long clubs, you will have a more horizontal swing. With the long clubs, take your trail arm and trail hand back as if you were carrying a serving tray. With the short irons and wedges, you will have a more vertical swing. With the short irons and wedges, take your trail arm and trail hand back as if you were carrying an umbrella.
- On the backswing, create an "L" between your lead forearm and your club shaft. Maintain this "L" for as long as possible on the downswing.

TOP OF THE SWING

- Your spine angle should remain the same as it was at address and your back should face the target—or at least face as close to the target as you can without changing your spine angle.
- On full shots, your wrists should be fully hinged and your clubhead should point toward the target. During the swing on full shots, the club should point toward the target five different times during the swing. The top of the swing is one of those times. (See Chapter 6: The Golf Swing for an explanation as to the five different times.)

DOWNSWING

- As stated earlier, the golf swing is a push-pull motion. You pull on the downswing. If you push on the downswing, your shots will be all over the place.
- As stated earlier, the golf swing is an up-and-down swing. On the downswing, swing down and then forward. If you swing down toward the ball instead of down, and then forward, you will probably hit the shot thin.
- In baseball, you want the knob of the bat to face the ball on the downswing. In golf, you want the butt end of the club to face down the target line on the downswing.
- On the downswing, pull the grip end of your club down with your lead arm as if you were jamming the butt of the club against an imaginary wall. Keep pulling the grip end of the club down all the way through the swing until the lead hand

reaches hip-high on the follow-through. While pulling the grip end of the club down and through, turn your belt buckle toward the target. This will have you getting your weight to the lead side on the downswing and follow-through, have you getting your hands to the ball before the clubhead, and have you hitting the ball farther than you ever have. (Thanks, SC!)

- When you are pulling the grip end of your club down and through (previous thought), know that when the clubhead is going down, your hands are actually going up. This is what keeps you from bottoming out and is what puts the speed of your swing in the clubhead and not the grip end. These two moves combined will have you hitting shots off the chart. (Thanks, RTG!)
- On the downswing, your trail shoulder goes under your chin. Keeping this thought in mind helps you stay down on the ball. Staying down on the ball is of the utmost importance.
- On the downswing, keep your chest down. If your chest is down, your club will be down.
- With the long clubs, start the downswing with your lower body (knees and hips). This will keep you from losing your balance and will allow you to swing down from the inside, in-to-square-to-in. If you start the downswing with your upper body, your arms and hands will take over the swing and you will swing outside-in, losing accuracy and possibly distance.
- With the short irons and wedges, the clubhead initiates the downswing. With the short irons and wedges it is more of an arms swing than a body swing. With the short irons and wedges, if you start the downswing with your lower body (knees and hips), you will most likely pull the shot.
- For straight shots straight down your target line, swing down from the inside, in-to-square-to-in. To swing down from the inside, your clubhead can never get outside the target line. To swing down from the inside, your hands must be closer to the target line than your clubhead until impact.
- On the downswing, keep your lead shoulder parallel or closed to the target line through impact. Keeping your lead shoulder parallel or closed to the target line will keep you from spinning out. Spinning out on the downswing will cost you both distance and accuracy.
- With all clubs other than your driver and putter, hit down on the ball. When you are hitting down on the ball, hit the ball and then the ground. If you hit the ground first, your ball is not going to go far and you may even injure yourself. If you don't hit the ground after you hit the ball, you are probably going to hit the shot thin, with low trajectory, possibly even a grounder. In golf, grounders are not what you want (unless you are putting).

- To help you get the feel for hitting down on the ball, visualize having to hit your shot over a body of water. To make the ball go up and over, you must hit down with much vigor.
- With all clubs other than your driver and putter, you want to take a divot on the target side of the ball. With the long clubs, you want to take a slight divot. With the middle irons, you want to take a mid-sized divot. With the short irons and wedges, you want to take a fairly good-sized divot.
- On the downswing, get your weight to the lead side. If you don't get your weight to the lead side on the downswing and follow-through, all the golf pointers in the world won't help you. (Thanks, SH!)
- To get your weight to the lead side on the downswing, visualize there is a ball two to five inches in front of your ball on the target side. Swing down as if that were the ball you were hitting.
- Swing through the ball and not to the ball. On full shots, remember that the ball is just the halfway point in your swing.

IMPACT

- At impact, with all clubs other than your driver and putter, the grip end of the club should be leaning slightly toward the target because you want to hit down on the ball.
- At impact, with your driver, the grip end of the club should be leaning away from the target and toward your zipper at impact. The grip end of the driver should be leaning away from the target because the ball is played forward in your stance and it is teed up. With your driver, you want to hit up on the ball. With your driver, if the grip end of the club is not leaning away from the target at impact, you will hit the ball on a low trajectory, probably costing you as much as twenty to thirty yards in distance.
- At impact, your trail wrist should still be hinged. You keep your trail wrist hinged by maintaining the "L" between your lead forearm and club shaft for as long as possible. The "L" I am speaking about is the "L" you created during your backswing. Revisit the last bullet under "Backswing" if needed.
- At impact, your lead arm should be pointing straight down toward the ground and in line with the inside of your lead leg.

RELEASING THE CLUB

- Release the club immediately after impact by releasing the "L" that you created between your lead forearm and your club shaft on the backswing.
- When you release the club, your trail shoulder should be down and both arms, along with your club shaft, should be fully extended and facing down the target line.

FOLLOW-THROUGH

- Keep turning toward the target.
- When the arms are parallel to the ground on the follow-through, in the three o'clock position, the grip end of the club should be pointing back toward your body. The toe of the club should be facing toward the sky.

FINISH

- Your finish should look like the top of your backswing reversed.
- At the finish, your trail shoulder should be closer to the target than your lead shoulder.
- To nail your finish, just before you start your backswing, you should focus on your finish. Are you going to finish with high hands or low hands? If you want to hit the ball high, play the ball forward in your stance, then start and finish with high hands. If you want to keep the ball lower, play the ball back in your stance, then start and finish with low hands.
- Hold your finish until the ball lands so that you can readily see what your ball did. If your ball did what you wanted it to do, remember what you did. If the ball didn't do what you wanted it to do, review Chapter 5: Ball Flight Laws. If Chapter 5 doesn't clear up why your ball did what it did, see Chapter 20: Faults and Fixes. If Chapter 20 doesn't give you a clear understanding as to why your ball did what it did, start back at the beginning of this book and work your way through again. I guarantee you, the answer to why your golf ball did what it did is in this book!

$\dfrac{8}{\text{CHAPTER}}$

DRAWINGS

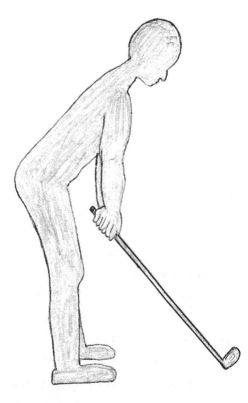

Drawing 8.1: Correct Posture

TO LEARN ALL ABOUT CORRECT POSTURE IN THE GOLF SWING, SEE "POSTURE" IN Chapter 4: Setup. As you will learn in that chapter, and as you can readily see in this drawing, at address, your arms should hang straight down and freely from your shoulder sockets.

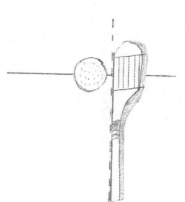

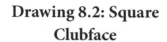

**Drawing 8.2: Square
Clubface**

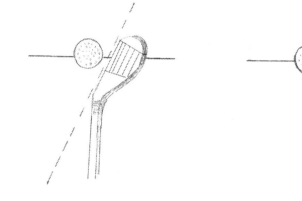

Drawing 8.3: Open Clubface   **Drawing 8.4: Closed
Clubface**

To hit straight shots straight down your target line, your clubface must be square to your target line at impact. If your clubface is open, you will hit a slice. If your clubface is closed, you will hit a hook. This concept is covered throughout the book.

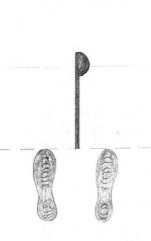

Drawing 8.5: Square Stance

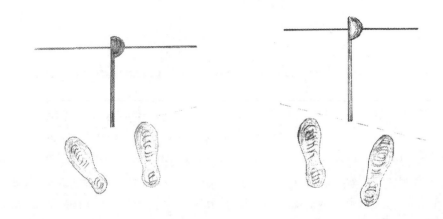

Drawing 8.6: Open Stance   **Drawing 8.7: Closed Stance**

To hit straight shots straight down your target line, your stance must be square to the target line at address and impact. If your stance is open, you will hit a slice. If your stance is closed, you will hit a hook. This concept is covered throughout the book.

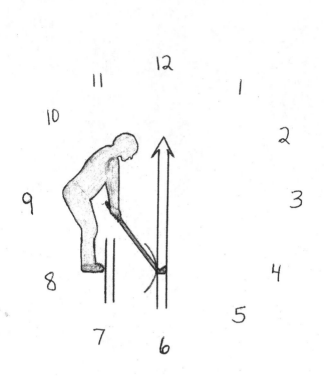

Drawing 8.8: Analog Clockface on the Ground for Target Line

For straight shots straight down your target line, when selecting a target line, visualize a set of railroad tracks. The ball, clubhead, and target are on the outside rail. Your shoulders, hips, knees, and feet are lined up parallel on the inside rail. For straight shots straight down your target line, your target line should be from six o'clock to twelve o'clock on an imaginary analog clockface lying on the ground. This imaginary analog clockface lying on the ground is lying on top of the outside rail of a set of imaginary railroad tracks. For straight shots straight down your target line, on the downswing, swing down from the inside, in-to-square-to-in, over this outside rail. To swing down from the inside, your clubhead can never get outside the target line. This concept is covered throughout the book.

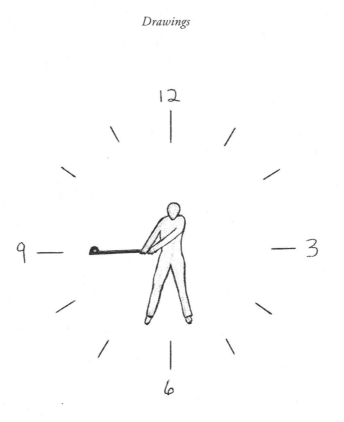

Drawing 8.9: Analog Clockface Behind Your Back for Determining Swing Length

Your distance is controlled by the length of your backswing. To get the feel for how far to take your hands back and through on a half swing, a three-quarters swing, and a full swing, think of having your back to an analog clockface with twelve o'clock above your head, nine o'clock to your right (for right-handed golfers), six o'clock at your feet, and three o'clock to your left (for right-handed golfers). On a half swing, swing your hands back to nine o'clock and then through to three o'clock. On a three-quarters swing, swing your hands back to ten o'clock and then through to two o'clock. On a full swing, swing your hands back to eleven thirty and then through to eleven thirty. When you are swinging your hands, your club will go back and through a little farther. Being able to hit each club to different distances by controlling the length of your backswing and follow-through can come in quite handy during a round of golf!

9
<u>CHAPTER</u>

CLUB SELECTION

When you are on the driving range, you can choose what type of shot you want to make and, therefore, which club you want to use. When you are playing a round of golf, the lie of the ball (where your ball came to rest from the previous shot) will determine what type of shot you need to make and, therefore, which club you should use. (For information as to what to do once you know your lie, see Chapter 10: Pre-Shot Routine.)

When playing a round of golf, you may carry up to fourteen clubs in your bag, including your putter. Which fourteen clubs you carry is a matter of personal preference, as long as they are deemed legal (for tournament purposes). The legal clubs you have to select from are driver, woods/metals, hybrids, long irons, mid irons, short irons, wedges, and putter. Because there are continually new and improved clubs on the market to select from, I am not going to attempt to tell you which clubs you should carry in your bag. Instead, I suggest you get with your local golf pro for guidance as to which clubs may be best for your current game. If you are going to need to purchase these clubs, again, I suggest that you get with your local golf pro and/or golf vendor.

Once you have obtained your clubs, the next thing you need to do is determine how far you hit each club in the air, excluding putter. You need to know how far you hit each club in the air in case you must hit the ball beyond trouble (water, ravine, bunker, etc.).

To determine how far you hit each club in the air, visit a driving range. After getting used to hitting each club somewhat consistently, you will probably come to find that you hit the clubs in the following order as to distance, farthest to shortest:

- Driver
- Fairway Wood/Metal

- Hybrid (aka Utility or Rescue Club)
- Long Irons (2-iron, 3-iron, 4-iron)
- Mid Irons (5-iron, 6-iron, 7-iron)
- Short Irons (8-iron, 9-iron, wedges)

When checking to see how far you hit each club in the air, you will probably find that when it comes to hitting your irons there is about a ten-yard difference between each club. In other words, you should be able to hit your 6-iron about ten yards farther than your 7-iron.

Also, realize that the lower the number on the club, the farther you should be able to hit the ball. The higher the number on the club, the higher and shorter you should hit the ball. In addition, know that most golfers can hit their woods/metals farther than their irons.

In addition, know that a lot of golfers have discontinued using long irons and have replaced them with hybrids because the hybrids are much easier to hit. Get with your local golf pro and/or golf vendor for guidance.

Just about every golfer carries a 3-wood/metal in their bag, which is smart. However, there are several other woods/metals that you may want to consider carrying as well (e.g., 5-wood/metal, 7-wood/metal, etc.), especially if you are a beginner or senior golfer. Some golfers, author included, state that they couldn't live without their 5-wood/metal and 7-wood/metal. Again, get with your local golf pro and/or golf vendor for guidance.

When it comes to wedges, you have many to choose from. The standard wedges are the pitching wedge (forty-eight degrees) and the sand wedge (fifty-six degrees). A lot of golfers have gone on to add a gap wedge (fifty-two degrees) and a lob wedge (sixty degrees plus). The wedges you choose are a matter of personal preference. Try the different wedges and then select the ones that work best for you and your game. When working/practicing with the different wedges, remember your goal is not to see how far you can hit the ball with each club, but how consistently you can hit the ball the needed distance with that particular club. After all, that is the reason for the different clubs.

When playing, before selecting the club for your shot, be sure to know the exact distance to the hole. If you are not on a tee box and don't have a rangefinder or something equivalent, remember the following:

- The blue stake is two hundred yards from the center of the green.
- The white stake is 150 yards from the center of the green.

- The red stake is one hundred yards from the center of the green.
- The sprinkler heads in the fairways usually will show the exact distance to the center of the green.

The pins are usually set up in the front, center, or back of the greens. There is usually about ten yards between each of these positions. Please check at the pro shop before you begin your round to determine where the pins are located on each green that day, if applicable.

If the pin is in the front, subtract ten yards from the distance indicated by the stakes (blue, white, red). If the pin is in the back, add ten yards. See "Approach Shot" in Chapter 12: Hitting Specialty Shots for pointers on where to land your shot, depending on which club you are using and the weather and ground conditions that day.

When selecting your club:

- Use the club that can get to the face of the ball best. On all shots, other than greenside bunker shots, you want to hit the face of the ball with the face of the club. If the ball is sitting down, you may have to go with an iron instead of a fairway wood to get to the face of the ball.
- Select the club based on the lie of the ball and then worry about the needed distance. If you are in a fairway bunker or are in the rough, your number one goal is to get out of the bunker or rough and get your ball back in play. You can make up for the needed distance on the next shot if needed.
- If you are between clubs for the distance you need, use one more club rather than trying to hit the lesser club harder and farther. For example, use your 5-iron rather than your 6-iron. You should be able to hit your 5-iron ten yards farther than your 6-iron. However, when going with this concept, ensure that you swing through to the finish—do not decelerate on your downswing because if you decelerate on your downswing, you will lose all control of your swing and the ball.
- If you need to hit a club a little shorter, you can add loft to your club by opening the clubface to your swing path. You open the clubface to your swing path by opening your stance. Remember, you will always swing along your shoulder line. Opening your clubface to your swing path will cause your ball to go higher and shorter. It will also cause the ball to land softer so you will get less roll. If you are a right-handed golfer, your shot will go a little right, so ensure that you aim a little farther left. Vice versa for left-handed golfers.
- Take one less club for every thirty-foot drop in elevation.
- Take one more club for every thirty-foot rise in elevation.

PRE-SHOT ROUTINE

YOUR WHOLE GAME IS BUILT AROUND YOUR PRE-SHOT ROUTINE. EVERY PROFESSIONAL golfer has a pre-shot routine, and you should have one as well. A good pre-shot routine helps you with consistency and helps eliminate outside thoughts. Outside thoughts will destroy your game. To hit a good shot, your entire focus needs to be on the shot you are about to make.

The following is a list of things you should do before making your shot. You don't want all of these thoughts running through your head just before you start your swing, but you may want to use these things as a checklist when you are practicing:

- ❏ If you are not on a tee box, check to see what kind of lie you have because the lie will determine which club you will need to use.
- ❏ Once you have checked the lie, visualize the shot you need to make. When visualizing the shot, visualize the trajectory, the carry (distance in the air), and the roll.
- ❏ Select the club for that shot. Select the club that will allow you to get to the face of the ball best. With all shots, other than greenside bunker shots, you want to hit the face of the ball with the face of the club.
- ❏ Select the club that allows you to get to the face of the ball best and then worry about the needed distance. You can make up for the needed distance on the next shot if needed.
- ❏ Before making your shot, take a few practice swings. When taking these practice swings, ensure that you duplicate the exact lie. For example, if your ball is on an uphill lie, make your practice swings from an uphill lie. If you are in a penalty area (water, ravine, bunker), you may not be able to ground your club when taking your practice swings. However, you still want to take practice swings. If

you have an uphill lie in a bunker, take your practice swings outside the bunker but on an uphill lie.

❑ When taking these practice swings, if your ball is not in a bunker, brush the ground on the backswing and the downswing. Note where your club brushes the ground on the downswing and play the ball just back of that spot so that you can make ball-first contact. Brush the ground in the same spot each time on the downswing—brushing the ground in the same spot will lead to consistency.

❑ Pay attention to the depth of your downswing. With the long clubs, if the ball is sitting up, you want to sweep the ball off the turf. With the long clubs, if the ball is not sitting up, you want to hit slightly down on the ball, taking a slight divot on the target side of the ball. With the middle irons (5-, 6-, 7-iron), you want to hit a bit more down on the ball, taking a mid-sized divot on the target side of the ball. With the short irons and wedges, you want to hit down steeply on the ball, taking a fairly good-sized divot on the target side of the ball.

❑ Grip the club lightly enough that you can feel the weight of the clubhead during your swing. If you can't feel the weight of the clubhead, you are gripping the club too tightly.

❑ Once you have completed your practice swings, walk behind your ball five to ten feet or so to determine your target line.

❑ Once you have selected your target line, don't take your eyes off of it. For this reason, walk up to your ball from behind it and not beside it.

❑ Set your clubface up to the ball and target line and then set your body up to your clubface. If you set your body up first, you will forever struggle with your game.

❑ For straight shots straight down your target line, set your body up square/parallel to your clubface and target line. For a fade, set up with an open stance. For a draw, set up with a closed stance. To better understand how to set up for these three distinct shots, see Chapter 12: Hitting Specialty Shots.

❑ When you set up to your clubface, your arms should be hanging straight down and relaxed from your shoulder sockets. Your hands should be hanging over your toe line. You should be looking in at your hands and not out at them.

❑ When you go to make the shot, fully realize that to hit straight shots straight down your target line, your clubface direction, your swing path, and your target line—all three—must match.

❑ Also fully realize that to hit straight shots straight down your target line, you must swing down the target line and not across it—you must swing down from the inside, in-to-square-to-in. To swing down from the inside, in-to-square-to-in, your clubface can never get outside your target line. If your clubface gets outside your target line, you will be swinging outside-in.

❑ To swing down from the inside, on the downswing, your hands must be closer to the target line than your clubhead until impact. Visualize slinging or swinging a ten-pound bag.

❑ Swing on plane. Your swing plane should match your club shaft angle at address.

❑ Focus on your finish position. Are you going to finish with high hands or low hands? To hit the ball high, play the ball forward in your stance and then start with high hands and finish with high hands. To keep the ball lower, play the ball back in your stance and then start with low hands and finish with low hands.

❑ Even though you want your last swing thought before you start your backswing to be on your finish position, don't forget to complete your backswing. If you don't complete your backswing, your ball is not going to go far because your distance is controlled by the length of your backswing. For long shots, take a long club and use a long backswing. For short shots, take a short club and use a short backswing. Do not decelerate on the downswing because if you decelerate on the downswing, you will lose all control of your swing and the ball.

❑ Swing through to the finish. If you don't swing through to the finish, you will probably not like where your ball finishes.

After using this checklist when you are practicing, create your own abbreviated pre-shot routine for when playing. A good pre-shot routine is a prerequisite for consistently hitting good shots because it will cause you to focus on your current shot.

11
<u>CHAPTER</u>

HITTING DIFFERENT CLUBS

IN THIS CHAPTER, I HAVE LISTED EACH TYPE OF CLUB AND INCLUDED THE SPECIFICS for hitting that particular club. Each time before going out to practice or play, look over these specifics to refresh your memory. Refreshing your memory could truly refresh your game!

HITTING DRIVER

- When hitting driver, you truly want to focus on making a good golf swing and just letting the ball get in the way because with driver, you are hitting the ball on the upswing.
- Tee the ball up so that half of the ball is above the top edge of your driver for more distance. Tee the ball lower for more accuracy.
- Play the ball in line with your lead heel.
- Have your hands even with the ball or a little behind the ball. If you have your hands ahead of the ball, you will deloft the club and hit a shot with a lower trajectory. This lower trajectory could cost you twenty or thirty yards.
- Have the grip end of the club shaft pointing at your zipper.
- Have the insides of your feet a little more than shoulder-width apart.
- For a straight shot, look at the back of the ball. For a slight draw, look at the back inside quadrant of the ball.
- For a straight shot, set up parallel to the six o'clock to twelve o'clock line on an imaginary analog clockface lying on the ground. See Drawing 8.8.
- For a fade (for right-handed golfers), set up parallel to the five o'clock to eleven o'clock line, with your clubface pointing at eleven thirty. See Chapter 12: Hitting Specialty Shots for additional pointers on how to hit a fade.

- For a draw (for right-handed golfers), set up parallel to the seven o'clock to one o'clock line, with your clubface pointing at twelve thirty. See Chapter 12: Hitting Specialty Shots for additional pointers on how to hit a draw.
- Have your weight 40/60 (lead foot/trail foot) at address.
- With your driver, the weight of the club is in the top portion of the clubhead, so you want to hit the ball with an ascending blow. To get the feel for this when you are out playing, take practice swings from an uphill lie. To get the feel for this when practicing, take your shoe off of your trail foot. Both of these drills will have your lead shoulder a little higher than your trail shoulder and improve your chances of hitting the ball with an ascending blow.
- Visualize you are slinging a bale of hay onto a low trailer. If you were slinging a bale of hay, you would be heavy on your feet and swing the bale back by turning your back to the target. You would then swing the bale forward using your lower body to help swing or sling the bale onto the trailer with an upswing. Remembering and mimicking this slinging motion when you are using your driver will help you stay grounded and will help you hit the ball on the upswing.
- On the downswing, swing parallel to the ground for about two feet and then hit the ball with an ascending blow. Visualize a small plane coming in and touching down on a runway and then taking back off again. Mimic that with your swing.
- Get your clubhead to the ball before your hands or at the same time. If your hands get to the ball first, you will deloft the club—and you will be hitting down on the ball.
- Keep your head and shoulders behind the ball. This will put more power in your swing.
- For more power and distance, play the ball a little more forward in your stance. This will force you to get your weight to the lead side on the downswing and follow-through.
- Usually the only time that you would use your driver is when you are hitting from a tee box. However, if you really need to hit a ball farther than you think you could with any other club in your bag, you may decide to try your driver somewhere other than the tee box. To hit your driver off of the fairway, ensure that you have a level or slightly uphill lie. Square the clubface to the target line and then open your stance to the target line. Opening your stance to the target line will add loft to the club because the clubface will be a little open at impact. Having your clubface a little open at impact will help you get the ball up a little bit. If you open

your stance to the target line, be sure and aim a little farther to your left (for right handed golfers) because the ball will tend to go to the right.

- If you are in trouble and need to keep the ball low yet hit it a long distance, you may want to use your driver. With this shot, don't open your stance to the target line because you don't want to add loft to your club—you want to keep the ball low.

HITTING FAIRWAY WOOD/METAL

- With the fairway wood/metal, let the lie dictate where you play the ball in your stance.
- From a good lie, play the ball farther forward in your stance and sweep it off the turf. To sweep the ball, take a few swings off to the side, observing where the clubhead brushes the ground on the downswing. This is where you should play the ball in your stance, which is typically a few inches inside your lead heel. This forward ball position helps promote a shallower approach, although the clubhead should still be moving slightly downward at impact. If you play the ball too far forward in your stance, you will thin the shot because your clubface will be coming up by the time it gets to impact.
- If the ball is sitting down, or you're hitting off hardpan, play the ball farther back in your stance and hit down on it. This will steepen your swing plane. The clubhead should contact the ball before reaching the bottom of its arc, imparting enough backspin to launch the ball up in the air with good distance.
- Look at the back of the ball.
- Have your hands a little ahead of the ball. The grip end of the club shaft should lean a little toward the target.
- Have the insides of your feet a little more than shoulder-width apart.
- Have a square, open, or closed stance, depending on what type of shot you are attempting to make. See the explanation under "Hitting Driver" as to how to set up to the ball for a straight shot, a fade, or a draw.
- Have your weight 50/50 (lead foot/trail foot) at address.
- Full extension through the shot is the key to nailing your fairway woods/metals. Keep the clubhead low to the ground after impact, extending your arms and club shaft down the target line for as long as possible.
- To make great contact with your fairway woods/metals, allow your arms to stretch out as you hit the shot. As your arms get longer, the club will make a wider arc,

plus the shaft will not lean severely behind the ball at impact. If the club shaft leans away from the target at impact, you will lose power and distance.

- Before you even get to the course, do some practice swings with your fairway wood/metal. Relax your arms and wrists. Feel the weight of the clubhead. As you do these practice swings, allow your arms to loosen up and try to make a wide arc when you swing the club down and through.

HITTING HYBRID (AKA UTILITY AND/OR RESCUE CLUB)

- Play the ball a little farther back in your stance than you would when hitting your woods/metals. Hitting a hybrid is more like hitting an iron than hitting a wood/metal.
- Have your hands a little ahead of the ball. The grip end of the club shaft should lean a little toward the target.
- Have the insides of your feet about shoulder-width apart.
- Have a square, open, or closed stance, depending on what type of shot you are attempting to make. See the explanation under "Hitting Driver" for how to set up to the ball for a straight shot, a fade, or a draw.
- Have your weight 50/50 (lead foot/trail foot) at address.
- At address, hover your club a little behind the ball instead of having your clubhead on the ground—this will remind you to hit down on the ball.
- Take a slight divot on the target side of the ball.

HITTING LONG IRON

- Play the ball a little farther back in your stance than you would when hitting your woods/metals.
- Look at the back of the ball.
- Have your hands a little ahead of the ball. The grip end of the club shaft should lean a little toward the target.
- Have the insides of your feet about shoulder-width apart.
- Have a square, open, or closed stance, depending on what type of shot you are attempting to make. See the explanation under "Hitting Driver" for how to set up to the ball for a straight shot, a fade, or a draw.
- Have your weight 50/50 (lead foot/trail foot) at address.

- Sweep the ball off the ground by taking a slight divot on the target side of the ball. Swing along the ground and not into the ground.
- To get the correct feeling for how to hit your long irons, place a thin towel on the ground an inch behind your ball. Swing down so that you hit the ball and not the towel. The secret to hitting the ball and not the towel is not in your hands and arms—it is in turning your big muscles (hips, core, shoulders) through the target and getting your weight to the lead side.

HITTING SHORT IRON

- Play the ball in the center of your stance. If you play the ball too far forward, you will pull it.
- Look at the front of the ball.
- Have your hands ahead of the ball. The grip end of the club shaft should point toward your lead thigh.
- Have a narrower stance.
- Have a slightly open stance—but keep your shoulders square (parallel) to the target line. Having a slightly open stance makes it easier to turn through the shot on the downswing.
- Have your weight on your lead side 60/40 (lead foot/trail foot) at address and keep it there throughout the swing.
- Make a three-quarters backswing with your arms—but remember to still turn your back to the target line.
- With the short irons (and wedges), your swing is more arm focused and less body oriented. With the short irons and wedges, the clubhead initiates the downswing—not the lower body. With the short irons and wedges, if you start the downswing with your lower body, your club will be thrown outside the target line, you will swing outside-in, and you will pull the ball.
- Swing down from the inside, in-to-square-to-in.
- Hit down on the ball. To help you get the feeling for hitting down on the ball, visualize hitting your shot over a body of water. To make the ball go up and over, you must hit down with much vigor.

12
CHAPTER

HITTING SPECIALTY SHOTS

DURING A ROUND OF GOLF, YOU WILL HAVE MANY OPPORTUNITIES TO HIT SPECIALTY shots. The more you know about these shots—and the more you practice them—the better you will be at making them.

TEE SHOT

- The only time you can tee a ball up is when you are hitting from a tee box. For this reason, most experienced golfers believe that you should take advantage of this rule and tee the ball up every time you are hitting from a tee box, even when you are using a short iron.
- When using a short iron, tee the ball low, possibly even as low as ground level. By having the ball on a tee, instead of on the ground, you will know for a fact that the ball is not sitting down in the turf. A ball sitting down is much harder to strike purely.
- When hitting the ball off a tee using a short iron, break the tee on your downswing. Breaking the tee when using a short iron confirms that you did indeed hit down on the ball. With short irons, you want to hit down on the ball and take a fairly good-sized divot on the target side of the ball. When using short irons and wedges, if you want the ball to go up, you must hit down.
- When using a driver off the tee box, no matter the size of the clubhead, tee the ball so that 50 percent of it is visible above the top edge of the clubface because you want to hit the ball with an ascending blow.
- When using any wood/metal other than your driver from the tee box, don't tee the ball too high; otherwise, you may swing under the ball and pop it up, losing valuable distance. On the other hand, if you want to take a little distance off of one of your woods/metals, tee the ball a little higher than normal. This will have

you hitting a shot with a higher trajectory, which should land softer and not roll as far. Doing this may keep your ball on the green on par 3's.

- When teeing the ball up, make sure you always tee up on the same side as trouble. Then, simply aim and hit away from the trouble. If you are slicing the ball when you are playing, tee the ball up on the far right side (for right-handed golfers) and aim far enough left so that even your biggest slice will find the fairway.
- On tight (narrow) fairways, you may want to tee the ball a bit lower for more accuracy. This may cost you some distance off the tee box, but by teeing the ball lower, hopefully your next shot will be from somewhere in the fairway instead of in the "junk." By being in the fairway, you can make up your lost distance on the next shot.

STRAIGHT SHOT STRAIGHT DOWN YOUR TARGET LINE

- Picture an analog clockface lying on the ground with the target line running from six o'clock to twelve o'clock, with six o'clock farther from the target. See Drawing 8.8.
- Have your shoulders, hips, knees, and feet parallel to the target line.
- Have your clubface pointing straight down the target line to twelve o'clock.
- On the downswing, swing down from the inside, in-to-square-to-in.
- To hit a straight shot straight down your target line, your clubhead can never get outside your target line on the downswing. If your clubhead gets outside your target line, you will be swinging outside-in.

FADE (CURVE TO THE RIGHT FOR RIGHT-HANDED GOLFERS)

- Play the ball a little forward in your stance—this will allow you to swing from outside-in.
- Picture an analog clockface lying on the ground with the target line running from six o'clock to twelve o'clock. Have your shoulders, hips, knees, and feet parallel to an imaginary line running from five o'clock to eleven o'clock. Have your clubface pointing to where the little hand on an analog clockface would be pointing at eleven thirty.
- Swing back and through along your shoulder line, five o'clock to eleven o'clock.
- Because your clubface is slightly open to your swing path, the ball will start out left of the target and will curve back toward the target (for right-handed golfers).
- When hitting a fade from the tee box, tee the ball a little lower because it helps you fade the ball.

- If you are not on a tee box, a tight lie (firm and/or short grass) favors a fade.
- Hitting a fade is easier with a flat club (a wood/metal).

DRAW (CURVE TO THE LEFT FOR RIGHT-HANDED GOLFERS)

- Play the ball back in your stance.
- Picture an analog clockface lying on the ground with the target line running from six o'clock to twelve o'clock. Have your shoulders, hips, knees, and feet parallel to an imaginary line running from seven o'clock to one o'clock. Have your clubface pointing to where the little hand on an analog clockface would be pointing at twelve thirty.
- Swing back and through along your shoulder line, seven o'clock to one o'clock.
- Because your clubface is slightly closed to your swing path, the ball will start out right of the target and will curve back toward the target (for right-handed golfers).
- When hitting a draw from the tee box, tee the ball a little higher because it helps you draw the ball.
- If you are not on a tee box, a lie where the ball is sitting up favors a draw.
- Hitting a draw is easier with a lofted club (an iron).
- On the downswing, drop your hands and arms down behind you—and not toward the ball.
- On the downswing, delay your shoulder rotation so that you don't spin out and/or come over the top.
- Release the club, closing the clubface, by rolling your trail forearm over your lead forearm. This rolling the trail forearm over begins when your arms are hip high on the downswing.

HIGH SHOT

- Don't have your hands too far in front of the ball because that delofts the club—causing you to hit the ball with a low trajectory.
- Open your stance a bit.
- Widen your stance a little by spreading your trail foot a few inches farther to the right (for right-handed golfers). This moves the ball forward in your stance and puts your upper body more behind the ball, helping you get the ball up.
- Even though you want to get the ball up, you still must hit down on the ball with all clubs other than your driver. For most golfers, if you try to pick the ball clean rather than hit down on it, you will forever struggle with your game. When you attempt to pick the ball clean, you may sometimes hit a beautiful shot. However, you will probably come to find that, just as often, you hit the ground behind the

ball or only hit the ball a third of the needed distance. It is hard to make consistent contact when you try to pick the ball clean.

- Start with high hands and finish with high hands. Swing high on the backswing and high on the finish. "To hit it high, reach for the sky!"

LOW RUNNING SHOT (STINGER)

- Use a 4-iron or 2-hybrid for long shots.
- Use a 7-iron if you need one hundred yards or less.
- Grip down on the club.
- Move your lead foot forward a little bit. This moves the ball back in your stance and will put your upper body farther to the lead side, helping you keep the ball low.
- Deloft the club by playing the ball back in your stance, off your trail toe. The lower you need to keep the ball, the farther back in your stance you play the ball.
- Close your stance a bit. This will help you swing down from the inside and will have you hitting a slight draw, which will lead to more distance.
- Close your clubface a bit.
- Stand closer to the ball.
- Cover the ball with your chest.
- Have your weight on the lead side 60/40 (lead foot/trail foot) at address and keep it there throughout the swing.
- Lean the grip end of the club forward.
- Visualize having your back to an analog clock. On the backswing, swing your hands back to eight o'clock. On the downswing, swing your hands through to five o'clock. When you swing your hands back and through, the clubhead will actually go a little farther.
- Hinge your wrists on the backswing but don't unhinge at impact. At impact, have the palm of your lead hand facing up with your lead knuckles facing down. This will ensure that you still have your trail wrist hinged.
- Keep your hands and the club shaft low after impact.

DOWNWIND SHOT (WITH THE WIND)

- Use a more lofted club.
- Make a full backswing and a full follow-through. This puts backspin on the ball, which gets the ball up and allows it to ride the wind.

UPWIND SHOT (AGAINST THE WIND)

- Play more club than you would normally use for that distance.
- Play the ball farther back in your stance—this will deloft the club a bit.
- Take a slower swing with a shorter backswing and shorter follow-through. This takes the backspin off the ball so it will travel lower through the wind.
- If you are on a tee box, tee the ball lower.

OVER TROUBLE

- Unless you are on a tee box and hitting your driver, make sure you hit down on the ball. If the ball is on the ground, you must hit down! If you don't hit down on the ball, you will probably hit the shot thin. If you hit the shot thin, the ball will probably not go over the trouble, but in.
- Have a slightly closed stance. This will help you swing down from the inside and will have you hitting a slight draw, which will lead to more distance.
- Set up with your weight on your lead side and keep it there throughout the swing.
- Stay grounded. Be heavy on your feet. Use your lower body.
- Stay in your posture by keeping your head steady.
- Turn back and through with your big muscles (shoulders, core, hips) by keeping your arms connected to your chest.
- Take a full swing—a full backswing, and then swing through to the finish.
- On the downswing, keep your lead shoulder closed or at least parallel to the target line through impact.
- Take a divot on the target side of the ball unless you are hitting your driver from a tee box.
- Hit through the ball and not to the ball.
- Make sure that you go long rather than come up short. You can probably play from long but possibly not from short.

FROM THE ROUGH

- If your ball is in light rough, you really don't have to change your technique. You merely need to allow for a possible flier, which can go about twenty yards farther than the same shot from the fairway. Use less club than you normally would.

- If the ball is in the rough but is sitting up, you can sweep the ball out with a 5-wood/metal or equivalent.
- If the ball is in the rough and is sitting down a little, use a 7-iron and swing with a somewhat steeper backswing and a low follow-through. You are merely trying to get the ball back into play while attempting to advance it as far as you can.

FROM DEEP ROUGH

- Play the ball back in your stance.
- Use your most lofted club—this will have you standing closer to the ball.
- Make a more upright backswing for a steeper attack angle into the ball. By coming down steeper on the ball, the ball is going to go higher.
- Use less club than you normally would for this distance because the ball will run farther since you will not be able to put backspin on it.
- Close the clubface a bit because the deep rough will open the clubface when you swing through.
- Grip the club more firmly so that the clubface doesn't open as dramatically when the grass grabs it.
- Don't ground your club. Rather, hover the clubhead above the rough so you don't catch grass on the backswing.
- Hinge your wrists quickly on your backswing. "If the rough is deep, you must swing steep."
- If your ball is in deep rough but is sitting up a bit, ensure that you don't swing under the ball and leave it in the rough.
- Hit down on the ball, trying to hit as close to the ball as you can.
- Make an aggressive swing through impact.

FROM A DIVOT

- Play the ball well back in your stance.
- Use a more lofted club because with the ball back in your stance, you will be delofting the club.
- Place a bit more weight on your lead side at address.
- Maintain your posture through impact.
- Make sure that you make ball-first contact.

FROM HARDPAN

- Play the ball back in your stance a bit.
- Use a less lofted club.
- Place a bit more weight on your lead side at address.
- Keep your hands in front of the clubhead and drive the leading edge into the ground just in front of the ball (target side). If you hit the ground first, the clubhead will bounce up, causing a thin or topped shot.

WITH BACKSPIN

- Ensure that the grooves in your clubface are clean and free of debris—it helps to have a clean ball as well, but that may be beyond your control.
- Play the ball in the center of your stance.
- Have your hands ahead of the ball.
- Have a little more weight on your lead side.
- Have a slightly open stance.
- Strike down and through the ball.
- To hit the ball low with backspin, take a short backswing and take a divot on the target side of the ball.
- To hit the ball high with backspin, have an open stance and swing from outside-in, along your shoulder line.

APPROACH SHOT

- First and foremost, notice the weather and ground conditions. Is the air heavy or light? Are the fairways and greens wet and slow or dry and fast? If the greens are hard, don't aim for the center of the green—instead, aim to come up a little short and let the ball roll to the hole.
- If the pin is at the front of the green, hit a high shot.
- If the pin is in the middle of the green, hit a ball with a normal trajectory. Land the ball about fifteen feet short of the pin and let the ball roll to the hole.
- If the pin is at the back of the green, hit a low shot so that the ball will roll all the way back to the hole.
- If the pin is on the right side of the green, aim for the center of the green with your clubface slightly open—the ball will hit the green and then roll to the right (for right-handed golfers).

- If the pin is on the left side of the green, aim for the center of the green with your clubface slightly closed—the ball will hit the green and then roll to the left (for right-handed golfers).
- If you can, leave your ball below the hole so that you will have an uphill putt just in case you don't sink the approach shot. Uphill putts are the easiest to make because you don't have to make a defensive putting stroke like you do on a fast, downhill putt.

13
CHAPTER

HITTING FROM UNEVEN LIES

EVERY UNEVEN LIE HAS A BALL FLIGHT TENDENCY. YOU MUST ALIGN AND ALLOW FOR that tendency. Whenever you are playing from an uneven lie, your goal is to keep the ball the same distance from your sternum and in the same place in your stance as if on a level lie.

UPHILL LIES
- Use one more club than you normally would from this distance because the ball is going to go higher since it is on an uphill lie. If you normally would use a 7-iron from this distance, use a 6-iron.
- Play the ball forward in your stance, off your lead leg.
- Have your shoulders at the same angle as the slope.
- Swing along the slope.
- On an uphill lie, the ball will always go to the left (for right-handed golfers), so aim a little right. The longer the shot, the farther right you should aim.

DOWNHILL LIES
- Use one less club than you normally would from this distance because the ball is going to stay lower and go farther. You will also get more roll, so be sure to allow for it.
- Grip down on the club.
- Play the ball in its normal position for that club. Don't play the ball back in your stance as it has been taught in the past (see the next bullet for explanation as to why).

- Have your shoulders at the same angle as the slope; this will move your sternum forward. This is why you position the ball in its normal position instead of playing it back in your stance.
- Swing along the slope.
- Step through the shot with your trail side.

WHEN THE BALL IS ABOVE YOUR FEET

- Play the ball back in your stance.
- Line the ball up with the heel of the club.
- Stand a little more erect.
- Grip down on the club—you want to shorten the club so it bottoms out in line with the slope. The steeper the slope, the more you want to grip down.
- Set your balance into the slope by having your weight on your toes, so you don't fall away.
- Aim more to the right of the target (for right-handed golfers) because the ball is going to go more to the left, especially with lofted clubs. The steeper the slope, the farther right you should aim.
- If the shot won't allow you to aim more to the right, then open your clubface but take one more club because the ball won't go as far with an open clubface.
- Make a flatter swing.
- Make a smooth swing.

WHEN THE BALL IS BELOW YOUR FEET

- Play the ball forward in your stance.
- Line the ball up more with the toe of the club.
- Use the full length of the club—grip the club near the end.
- Bend more from the hips.
- Flex your knees more so that you can stand closer to the ball.
- Put more weight on your heels to avoid falling down the slope.
- Aim more to the left of the target with long clubs (for right-handed golfers) because the ball is going to go more to the right. The more loft you have on the club, the less the ball will cut so you don't have to aim as far left. Aim fifteen yards left for a 4-iron; three to four yards left for pitching wedge.
- Use less body movement—swing with your arms and hands.
- You will have more of an upright swing, so be sure to keep your chest down over the ball.

- Let the club come down to impact with an open face—don't try to close the face. Trying to close the face will result in you falling down the slope.
- To keep your balance, your follow-through will be restricted. Since this will most likely decrease the distance that your ball will travel, use plenty of club. If you would normally use a 7-iron for this distance, use a 6- or a 5-iron.

In summary:

- When the ball is above your feet, aim more to the right (for right-handed golfers) because the ball is going to go left; when the ball is below your feet, aim more to the left (for right-handed golfers) because the ball is going to go right. A great way to remember which way the ball is going to go when the ball is above or below your feet is to visualize rolling the ball from where it lies along the slope. If the ball is above your feet, the ball is going to roll left (for right-handed golfers). If the ball is below your feet, the ball is going to roll right (for right-handed golfers).
- Even though the pointers above are factual, if you allow the heel of your club to come into the shot first, you are probably going to pull the shot. In that case, you can throw the previous pointer out the window. To keep from pulling the shot when you come into the ball on the downswing, ensure that the toe and the heel come in evenly (level) and at the same time.

HITTING FROM FAIRWAY BUNKERS

- If the lip is a problem, use a club with more loft. In a bunker, your number one priority is to get the ball out and back in play while advancing it as far as you can.
- If the lip is no problem, think of the club you would use from the same distance from off the grass and then choose one more club.
- Take a practice swing (or two) outside the bunker, matching the same slope angle you have in the bunker.
- Dig your feet into the sand to give yourself a stable base.
- Grip down on the club to offset digging your feet into the sand.
- Be careful not to flex your knees too much because you want to stand taller on fairway bunker shots.
- Lean forward.
- Pick the ball clean. If you catch the sand, the ball will not go far.
- When hitting a wood/metal, open your stance, play the ball in line with your lead heel, open your clubface a bit, and then aim a little left of your target (for right-handed golfers) because you will hit a slight fade (your ball will curve back to the right).
- When hitting an iron, close your stance, play the ball in the center of your stance, close the clubface, and then aim a little right of your target (for right-handed golfers) because with a closed stance and a closed clubface, you will hit a slight draw (your ball will curve back to the left).
- Keep your lower body quiet.

HITTING FROM GREENSIDE BUNKERS

BEFORE HITTING FROM A GREENSIDE BUNKER THERE ARE SEVERAL THINGS YOU NEED to consider: the lie, the lip, the type of sand, and the distance you need the ball to travel. Each of these factors has its own unique problems and solutions.

Next, you need to determine whether you are going to have an open or closed clubface and whether you are going to have an open or closed stance (swing path) because these things determine the trajectory and length of the shot.

If you need to hit a high, short shot, open the clubface a lot and open your stance a lot. If you need to hit the ball farther, don't open your stance or the clubface as much. No matter whether you have an open stance and/or open clubface or not, aim directly at the pin.

On greenside bunker shots, never hit the ball. Instead, throw sand out of the bunker and let the ball ride out on the sand.

To hit good sand shots, use the bounce of your club, not the leading edge (unless so specified). Clubs with a lot of bounce work best in soft, powdery sand. For fluffy sand, use your sand wedge and slide the bounce of the club through the sand under the ball.

Clubs with less bounce work best in coarser sand. For firm sand, use your pitching wedge.

Soft sand—hard swing. Hard sand—soft swing, but still follow through. Wet sand—soft swing, but still follow through.

On hard, wet sand, keep the clubface a little squarer rather than opening the blade. On the downswing, come down steeper to force the blade through the sand underneath the ball. Doing this will keep you from thinning the shot.

At address, hold the leading edge of the club directly over the spot where you plan for it to enter the sand. The closer you hit to the ball, with less sand, the farther the ball will fly.

Throw sand out of the bunker and the ball will come with it. If you don't throw sand out of the bunker, the ball will probably not come out.

Turn your chest through the shot and extend your arms through the shot.

Never stop your swing when you are in a bunker. If you stop your swing in a bunker, the ball will probably not come out.

PLAYING FROM AN UPHILL LIE

- Use your sand wedge.
- Play the ball forward in your stance.
- Open your stance.
- Open the clubface before you grip the club, so that the clubface is pointing toward the sky.
- Have your weight on your lead side.
- Have your hands in the center of your stance. Don't have your hands in front of the ball because that delofts the club.
- Take a steep backswing by hinging your wrists quickly.
- On the downswing, swing the club along your body line and not the target line. With your clubface open and your stance open, they offset each other, so the ball will go straight.
- With soft sand, swing hard and swing all the way through. If you stop your swing short, the ball may not get out of the bunker.
- Ensure that the bottom edge (the bounce of your sand wedge) goes through the sand first, not the leading edge of the club. If the leading edge goes through the sand first, your club will bury/stop, and the ball probably will not come out of the bunker.
- The closer you hit to the ball, the farther the ball will go.
- Your goal is to send the sand onto the green with the ball, so feel how much effort it would take to propel the sand out of the bunker. When there's only a little sand,

or it's firm and tight, you don't need much effort. When there's a lot of sand, or it's fluffy and heavy, you need to make a bigger swing.

PLAYING FROM A LEVEL LIE

- Use your sand wedge.
- Play the ball in the center of your stance.
- Open your stance.
- Open the clubface before you grip the club. If you need the ball to go farther, don't open your stance or the clubface as much.
- Have your weight on your lead side.
- Don't have your hands in front of the ball because that delofts the club.
- Take a steep backswing by hinging your wrists quickly.
- On the downswing, swing the club along your body line and not the target line. With your clubface open and your stance open, they offset each other, so the ball will go straight.
- On a short shot—swing easy—visualize a second baseman throwing to first. On a longer shot—swing harder—visualize a third baseman throwing to first. The throwing motion looks the same as with the second baseman—it's the speed of the arm swing that changes the power of the throw.
- When coming down into the ball, visualize that the ball is lying in a soup bowl. Scoop down and through the depth of a soup bowl.

PLAYING FROM A DOWNHILL LIE

- Use your pitching wedge.
- Play the ball back in your stance.
- Open your stance.
- Square the clubface.
- Have your weight on your lead side.
- Have your hands in front of the ball.
- Take a steep backswing by hinging your wrists quickly.

PLAYING FROM A BURIED LIE

- When you find your ball buried in the sand, you must adjust your approach. Instead of trying to glide the club through the sand under the ball, you want to pick the club up abruptly and bury the club into the sand behind the ball with a lot of force. Swing down as if you were chopping down a tree with an ax. Bury the ax in the sand. This will cause the ball to pop out.

- Use your pitching wedge.
- Play the ball back in your stance.
- Open your stance.
- Close the clubface considerably because when you chop down into the sand, the sand will somewhat open the clubface.
- Have your weight balanced over your feet.
- Have your hands in front of the ball.
- Take a steep backswing.

16
<u>CHAPTER</u>

THE SHORT GAME

THE SHORT GAME CONSISTS OF PUTTING, CHIPPING, AND PITCHING. MASTERING THESE three aspects of your game can do wonders for your game.

Whether your next shot will be a putt, chip, or pitch should be determined when you get closer to the green. No matter whether you are going to putt, chip, or pitch, you should be surveying the green when you are approaching it. Surveying the green enables you to get a better feel for which way the green breaks and, therefore, which way your ball will roll once it gets on the green.

To be great around the greens, you need to control contact, trajectory, and roll. With putts, chips, and pitches, your hands pretty much stay below your waist, and you keep your lead wrist straight and firm throughout the swing. Don't flip your wrists or cast your club!

When you are deciding whether to putt, chip, or pitch, remember:

- When you can putt, putt.
- When you can't putt, chip.
- When you can't chip, pitch.

PUTTING
- Read the putt from behind the hole, from the low side of the putt, and from behind the ball.
- When reading the putt, get down to ground level so that you can truly get the read. If you have trouble getting down to ground level, walk farther back behind the ball. The farther back you walk, the better read you will get.

- To determine how hard to hit the putt, and which line to choose, visualize rolling the ball with your bare hands. Visualize how hard you would roll it and which line you would choose. Choose the same speed and line with your putter.
- When making your decisions regarding the putt, decide on the speed that you are going to roll the putt first and then decide on the line. The speed at which you are going to roll the putt will always determine the line.
- Speed is the biggest factor in putting. Good speed with a bad line almost always puts you closer to the hole than bad speed with a good line.
- When putting, picture the line and then ensure that your putter face is square with that line at impact. Having your putter face square to your target line is 90 percent of the battle in sinking putts. To help you square your putter face at impact, imagine that your ball is sitting on top of a credit card that is square to your target line. Swing your putter face down and through the credit card (and target line).
- Know that for you (the golfer), all putts are straight putts. Even though the putt may break—you must hit a straight putt. You hit a straight putt and let the break take the ball to the hole. If you try to pull or push a putt, you will forever struggle.
- Please know that when you hit putts gently, gravity has more time to work, so you need to play more break. However, also know, the slower the green speed, the less a putt will break.
- In the winter, putts will usually not break as much because the greens are usually slower that time of the year.
- The more uphill the putt, the less the putt will break.
- If you are putting against the grain (the grass looks dull), the ball will roll slower and break less.
- If you are putting with the grain (grass looks shiny), the ball will roll faster and break more.
- The faster the green speed, the more the putt will break.
- The more downhill the putt, the more the putt will break.
- The break will usually go away from bunkers for maintenance purposes because if the break is away from the bunker, there will be less work involved in maintaining the bunker. Remember this fact when you are trying to determine the break.
- When you have a breaking putt, don't aim at the hole or the apex—aim higher. The ball will roll over the apex, but you don't aim for the apex. If you aim for the apex, the putt will always end up below the hole.
- On breaking putts, it is better to misaim on the high side because a misaimed putt, or a mishit putt, may accidentally roll down and drop into the cup. A putt that misses on the low side of the cup never has a chance to go in.

- If you cannot determine which way the putt breaks, aim for the center of the cup. That way you have a fifty-fifty chance of making a good putt. (Thanks, MC!)
- Don't get over the ball until you are sure of the line. Once you find the line, don't take your eyes off of it.
- When putting, keep your eyes trained on the hole and the line that you have chosen. Don't overly worry about body positions or how precise your aim is. Your body and mind will naturally adjust and make it happen if you're looking at the target line.
- Focus on making the putt rather than focusing on technique. If you focus on technique, you may master the technique but fail to sink the putt.
- Great putters never think about mechanics; instead, they think about making the putt.
- Never come up short on a putt because you miss 100 percent of those putts.
- On uphill putts, aim for the back of the cup. On downhill putts, hit them softly enough that the ball will trickle down and fall into the cup.
- When playing the ball from off the green, strike the ball firmly enough to at least get the ball onto the green. If you don't, you will have the same shot all over again.
- When playing the ball off the fringe, stroke the putt firmly enough to get the ball through the fringe, but realize that the ball will begin rolling faster once it gets onto the green. The ball will probably also break a little one way or the other when it gets onto the green so be sure and allow for that.
- When playing the ball off the fringe, play the ball in the center of your stance instead of forward. This helps you to strike down more than you do with a putt on the green.
- When you putt on the green, you don't want to hit down on the ball because the ball will hop before it starts to roll. With the putter, you want to hit the top half of the ball much like you would hit a tire if you were rolling it down the road. This keeps the ball (and the tire) on the ground and keeps it rolling steady.

Putting Stance

- The putter should be an extension of your lead arm.
- Stick your arms straight out. Then bend from the waist until your arms hang vertically. When putting, bend from the waist. (With all other clubs, bend from the hips.)
- Have your hands directly under your shoulders.
- The ball should be directly under your lead eye.
- At address and throughout the stroke, your eyes must be directly over the ball. If your eyes are inside the ball, your view of the target is distorted, and it's likely

you'll line up pointing to the right (for right-handed golfers). If your eyes are outside the ball, you'll probably line up to the left (for right-handed golfers).

- Have your shoulders and forearms parallel to the putting line because the path of your putter will follow the line of your shoulders and forearms.

Putting Stroke

- Use your shoulders and arms.
- Keep your shoulders and forearms parallel to the target line.
- Rock your shoulders back and forth.
- Keep your lead wrist firm and straight.
- Eliminate any wrist action because there is no way that you can make consistent contact if you hinge and unhinge your wrists. When you hinge and unhinge your wrists, you may hit the ball softly and come up short one time, and at another time, you may strike the ball firmly and roll it off the green. Again, eliminate any wrist action when putting.
- Keep your head still.
- Keep your lower body steady—but not rigid.
- Keep the putter face square to the target line at impact because the face angle at impact is responsible for at least 90 percent of your putting success.
- Make a couple of practice strokes to give you a feel for the distance. Do this even on short putts because it will keep you from jabbing at the ball and/or decelerating during your stroke.
- Accelerate through the ball on all putts, excluding fast downhill putts. If you decelerate during the putt, you will lose all control of the stroke and the ball.
- On all putts, follow through with the putter head facing down the target line or you will forever push your putts.
- Make sure you hit the sweet spot on your putter (the center). If you don't hit the sweet spot, you will lose distance and direction.
- To help you hit the sweet spot each time, keep your eyes on the ball and keep your head down throughout the putt. To help you with this, visualize a coin under your ball. After you have made the stroke, you have to be able to tell whether the coin is on heads or tails.
- Stay down on the putt. If you raise up, you will push the ball. If you open your lead shoulder, you will pull the ball.
- Keep the same tempo on long putts as you do on short putts. Distance is controlled by the length of your backswing and follow-through—not effort.
- Don't play the ball too far forward in your stance—or you will lose control of your swing and push the putt.

On Short Putts
- Direction is more important than distance.
- Grip your putter lower on the shaft.
- Take the putter straight back and straight through.
- Hug the ground with your putter while going back and going through.
- Aim for inside the cup and strike the ball firmly enough to hold the line.

On Long Putts
- Distance is more important than direction.
- Position the ball in line with your lead heel.
- Take the club back to the inside. Swing down from the inside, squaring the putter face to the target line at impact.
- Don't try to hit the ball harder—simply make a longer backswing and a longer follow-through.
- Accelerate through the ball with your trail arm.

On Fast Downhill Putts

On fast, downhill putts, try making virtually no stroke; merely take the putter back an inch or so and then tap the ball. The ball will begin to roll and gravity will take care of the rest.

Putting Wisdom

When putting, never concern yourself with the outcome of the putt because that is beyond your control. Some putts will mysteriously go in, and others will mysteriously stay out. The only thing you can control is your stroke. Make a good stroke, and more times than not, good things will happen!

CHIPPING

A chip shot is just an extension of a putt and is played with anything from a 4-iron to a wedge. A chip shot is a short shot that's mostly on the ground. The biggest difference between a chip shot and a pitch shot is the spin. On a chip shot, you have no backspin on the ball, so it will roll. With a chip shot, the basic idea is to get the ball on the green and rolling as soon as you can, because if you can get the ball rolling like a putt, judging how far it will go is a lot easier.

As stated earlier, to be great around the greens, you need to control contact, trajectory, and roll. With putts, chips, and pitches, your hands pretty much stay below your waist, and you keep your lead wrist straight and firm throughout the swing. Don't flip your wrists or cast your club!

To keep your lead wrist straight on the downswing and follow-through when chipping, on the follow-through, the grip end of the club should point to the left of your lead hip (for right-handed golfers) and not back toward your body. If the grip end of the club is pointing back toward your body, you are flipping your wrists. Flipping your wrists is not what you want to do!

When chipping, on the downswing, pull the grip end of the club down as if you were jamming the butt end of the club against an imaginary wall. Keep pulling the grip end of the club down all the way through the swing until the lead hand reaches hip-high on the follow-through.

To get the feel for how to keep your lead wrist straight on the downswing and follow-through when chipping, extend an alignment stick past the grip end of your club. When you swing down and through, the alignment stick should not bump up against your lead hip. Instead, it should point to the left of your lead hip (for right-handed golfers).

When deciding whether to chip or pitch, always chip if:

- The lie is poor.
- The green is hard.
- You have a downhill lie.
- The wind has an influence on the shot.
- You are under stress/pressure.

When chipping, if you want to keep the ball low:

- Play the ball back in your stance. The lower you want to keep the ball, the farther back you play it.
- Keep your lead wrist firm and straight.
- Don't hinge your trail wrist on the backswing or downswing.

When chipping, if you want more air under the ball:

- Play the ball forward in your stance.
- Keep your lead wrist firm and straight.
- Hinge your trail wrist on the backswing but not on the downswing.

If you are chipping from the fringe, use your putting stance and your putting motion. When chipping from the fringe, also consider the following:

- Use your 5-iron.
- Play the ball back in your stance.
- Slightly open your stance—but keep your shoulders parallel to the target line. Slightly open your stance so that you can swing down the target line more easily.
- Aim the clubface square to the ball and target line.
- Take a short, slow, and even swing with no wrist break on the backswing or the downswing.
- Remember that the ball will roll faster once it gets onto the green, so allow for that when you make your stroke.

For all other chip shots, consider the following:

- Your feet should be close together.
- Your stance should be open, but your shoulders must be parallel to the target line. Opening your stance makes it easier to swing down the target line. Keeping your shoulders parallel improves your chances of swinging down the target line.
- Your weight should be on your lead foot with your head down.
- Your hands should be ahead of the ball—and your hands must lead.
- On the downswing, the knees pivot toward the target.
- Keep the rhythm the same for all lengths of shot; simply vary the length of your backswing for more distance.
- Swing down a little from the inside and down the target line. If you swing down across the ball (outside-in), you will slice the ball every time.

In determining which club to use when chipping, always consider:

- The lie of the ball. When you are on hard, bare ground, never use a wedge because the danger of thinning or fluffing the shot outweighs any advantage gained. Reach instead for a straighter-faced club to make the shot.
- The distance between the ball and the pin. When there is less green between your ball and the pin, use a club with more loft. When there is a lot of green between your ball and the pin, use a club with less loft.
- The ground conditions on the green. If the green is firm, you will get more roll. If the green is wet and/or soft, your ball will probably slow immensely. Use the

"Rules of Thumb on Roll When Chipping" to help you determine which club to use based on the ground conditions.

- For bump-and-run chip shots, use a 7-iron for longer shots. Use a 9-iron for inside ten yards.

<u>Rules of Thumb on Roll When Chipping</u>
Sand Wedge (1:1): one part carry, one part roll.
Pitching Wedge (1:2): one part carry, two parts roll.
9-iron (1:3): one part carry, three parts roll.
8-iron (1:4): one part carry, four parts roll.
7-iron (1:5): one part carry, five parts roll.
6-iron (1:6): one part carry, six parts roll.

These "Rules of Thumb on Roll When Chipping" are based on the premise that you land your chip shot one to three feet onto the green. However, sometimes you will want to land the ball short of the green and let the fringe take some of the speed off of the ball. This technique is usually used if you are using a club with less loft, such as your 7-iron, 6-iron, or 5-iron.

When chipping, the closer you are to the level of the flag, the more you can afford to choose a direct line to the hole. However, you still need to allow for a bit of break once your ball lands on the green.

When you have a green that slopes from one side to the other, the first thing you need to remember is that the actual target line is no longer a straight line to the pin. The actual target line is above the hole. When hitting chip shots onto a green that slopes, use the same wisdom that was shared about breaking putts. On breaking putts, as well as chips, it is better to misaim on the high side because a misaimed putt/chip—or a mishit putt/chip—may accidentally roll down and drop into the cup. A putt/chip that misses on the low side never has a chance to go in.

In addition, you want to remember, even though this seems contradictory to the previous pointer, if you don't sink this shot, you want to leave the ball below the hole if possible because uphill putts are a lot easier to make than downhill putts. With uphill putts, you don't have to make a defensive stroke.

Determining which club to use and where to play the ball in your stance takes practice. Before doing this practice, familiarize yourself with the principles in this chapter and with the "Rules of Thumb on Roll When Chipping."

Another great way to help you determine which club to use is to lay your club down on the ground with the clubface facing up and then step on the clubface so that the club shaft rises off the ground. The angle that the club shaft points at is the angle that your ball will fly when struck during your chipping motion. If you need a higher trajectory, choose a club with more loft, which will be a club with a higher number. When making this decision, remember the carry-to-roll ratio. See "Rule of Thumb on Roll When Chipping."

When it comes to chipping, one of the key things you need to know is that your weight should be on your lead foot at address and should stay there throughout the swing. If your weight is on your trail foot, the leading edge of the club will be coming up at impact. That is not a good thing.

When it comes to chipping, the next important thing to know is that you have to decide whether you are going low or high. If you are going low, the ball will be played in line with your trail foot. If you are going high, the ball will be played in line with your lead foot. If you want to go really low, play it farther back in your stance. If you want to go really high, play it farther forward in your stance. Whatever you do—never play it in the center of your stance.

When playing a chip shot, you have four options. These four options are listed from easiest to hardest. For the sake of your game and your score, whenever you can, select Option 1. Also, for the sake of your game and your score, practice each of these options because during the course of your golfing career, you will probably get an opportunity to use all four.

Chipping Options

Option 1: You would rather chip the ball off your back foot with a square clubface. However, with this option, you will get a lot of roll.

Option 2: To reduce the roll, play the ball off your back foot with a slightly open clubface.

Option 3: If that will still give you too much roll, play the ball off your lead foot with a square clubface.

Option 4: To reduce the roll even more, play the ball off your lead foot with an open clubface.

When chipping from a downhill lie:

- Use your sand wedge.
- Play the ball forward in your stance.
- Have your shoulders parallel to the slope; this will move your sternum forward. That is why you position the ball forward in your stance.
- Pick up the club quickly with plenty of wrist break to follow the contours of the slope. This will help the ball gain height.
- Use the bounce of your sand wedge to glide through the grass.

When chipping up to a two-tier green, it is best to use the bump-and-run technique. When using the bump-and-run up a two-tier green, hit the ball firmly enough to get up to the second tier.

When chipping down a two-tier green, use a lofted club and a delicate chip. You want to hit the ball with just enough speed so that it almost comes to rest at the top of the downslope. From there, gravity takes over and takes the ball down toward the hole.

PITCHING

A pitch shot is used when you need the ball to fly high in the air, possibly over a hazard. Pitch shots are played only with a wedge or a 9-iron. Please remember, the only time you want to use your sand wedge for a pitch shot is when the ball is on a soft, grassy lie.

Since a pitch shot is longer than a chip shot, you need to make a longer swing and hinge your trail wrist on the backswing. On a pitch shot, you will have a lot of backspin on the ball. However, remember, you can't get much spin on the ball in wet conditions or from the rough. You also probably will not get much spin if the ball is dirty or muddy.

As stated earlier, to be great around the greens, you need to control contact, trajectory, and roll. With putts, chips, and pitches, your hands pretty much stay below your waist, and you keep your lead wrist straight and firm throughout the swing. Don't flip your wrists or cast your club!

To keep your lead wrist straight on the downswing and follow-through when pitching, on the follow-through, the grip end of the club should point to the left of your lead hip (for right-handed golfers) and not back toward your body. If the grip end of the club is pointing back toward your body, you are flipping your wrists—and flipping your wrists is not what you want to do.

To get the feel for how to keep your lead wrist straight on the downswing and follow-through when pitching, extend an alignment stick past the grip end of your club. When you swing down and through, the alignment stick should not bump up against your lead hip. Instead, it should point to the left of your lead hip (for right-handed golfers).

When deciding whether to chip or pitch, you probably want to pitch the ball if:

- The lie is good.
- The green is soft.
- You have an uphill lie.
- There is an obstacle (bunker, water, or ravine) in the way.

When pitching from an uphill lie, use a less lofted club because the uphill lie adds loft. If you don't remember this fact when pitching, your shot is probably going to come up short.

When visualizing your pitch shot, imagine pitching the ball underhanded onto the green. How high would you loft it—and how hard would you throw it?

When pitching, let your knees provide the rhythm. Visualize pitching the ball underhanded and visualize how much you would use your knees. Use this same motion when pitching the ball with your pitching wedge.

When pitching, the distance of the ball from the feet slightly increases as the length of the shot increases, and the arms and shoulders swing back farther as the shot being played gets longer. In each case, the hands and arms are working together to create a square impact. The head is held steady and the weight of the lower body moves onto the lead side, with the shoulders becoming square to the ball at impact. The spine angle is maintained through impact.

When hitting pitch shots, you don't want to come up short. To avoid coming up short, make sure you don't decelerate and/or quit on the downswing and follow-through.

General guidelines on pitching:

- Open your stance.
- Open the clubface before you grip the club on most pitches.
- Hinge your wrists early on the backswing.

- Turn your body back and through.
- Keep looking down at the lie after the ball has left the clubface. This will keep you from lifting.

To get your pitches to bite:

- On your backswing, point your thumbs at the sky and the butt of the club at the ground.
- Come down sharply into the ball to get it rolling up the clubface.
- Once you feel impact, stop your hands abruptly at waist height and keep them and your club low. The faster you accelerate and then stop, the more spin you will put on the ball.

When pitching from a downhill lie, close to the green:

- Use your most lofted wedge.
- Open your stance.
- Open the clubface completely before you grip the club. Have the clubface pointing toward the sky.
- Swing along the slope.
- Swing along your body line.

When making a short pitch over a hazard:

- Use your sand wedge or pitching wedge.
- Open your stance.
- Aim the clubface at the pin.
- Aim to drop the ball on the top of the flag; this will have the ball coming in and landing softly.
- Hinge your wrists early on the backswing.

When hitting a lob shot (high floater pitch shot):

- Use your most lofted wedge.
- Play the ball forward in your stance—even with your lead heel.
- Open your stance.
- Open the clubface completely before you grip the club. Have the clubface pointing toward the sky.
- Hinge your wrists early on the backswing while maintaining the open clubface.

- Keep the clubface open throughout the swing—and don't let the clubface turn over on the follow-through.
- Have the bounce of your club go under the ball first rather than the leading edge of your club.
- Swing down and through as if you were attempting to knock the legs off of a table.
- Swing through keeping your hands and the clubface low to the ground after impact.
- On the follow-through, keep the clubface open and pointing toward the sky.

17
CHAPTER

GOLF WISDOM

Even though you play the game from the tee box to the green, you want to practice the game from the green to the tee box. Please see Chapter 19: Practice Thoughts and Drills as to why.

When you practice, work on your swing. When you play, work on your game.

Each time before you play a round of golf, practice your short game for a bit. When I am talking about practicing your short game, I am talking about putting, chipping, and pitching—not just putting!

Each time before you play a round of golf, hit a few full shots so that you can see what your tendencies are that day. Everyone has tendencies and they do seem to change from day to day. When playing that day, don't try to fix your tendencies; instead, simply allow for and/or capitalize on them.

If you haven't been club fitted, know that your clubs may be too long for you. If your clubs are too long for you, simply grip down on them so you don't bottom out during your downswing. Bottoming out will cost you distance and can even lead to injury. Please see Chapter 3: Grip for how to determine what depth you should grip your club.

The most important shot in golf is the one you are about to make. It doesn't matter how well, or not-so-well, you hit the previous shot. That shot is over. To hit a good shot now, your entire focus must be on this shot.

When playing, don't worry about mechanics. Simply visualize the shot. Your mind and body will make it happen. When visualizing the shot, visualize the trajectory, the carry (distance in the air), and the roll.

If you want to make birdies, distance is more important than direction. If your second shot has to be longer than your first (tee shot), making birdies becomes a bit more difficult. In addition, know that you can't birdie them all if you don't birdie the first one!

Your distance is controlled by the length of your backswing, which includes the length of your club. For long shots, take a long club and use a long backswing.

You can add distance to a club by delofting it—by playing the ball farther back in your stance. If you deloft your club, remember to allow for more roll once the ball lands.

You can reduce distance in your shot by playing a fade rather than a straight shot or a draw. A straight shot and a draw will roll farther after landing than a fade. See Chapter 12: Hitting Specialty Shots for information on how to hit all three of these shots.

Never come up short on any shot because any time you come up short it will cost you at least one more stroke. (Thanks TK!) The only time you would consider coming up short is if going long would put you in trouble. Before taking your shot, weigh the pros and cons of going long versus coming up short.

Tee the ball high for more distance. Tee the ball lower for more accuracy.

On tee shots, when hitting with the wind, use your 3-wood/metal instead of your driver. The 3-wood/metal will launch the ball higher and let the ball just ride the wind.

On a hole where there is trouble, you should think of accuracy rather than distance. If it is going to take a perfect shot to go over trouble (water, ravine, or bunker), choose to land your ball somewhere else.

If you need to go over trouble:

- Have more of your weight on your lead side at address and keep it there throughout the swing.
- Unless you are on a tee box and hitting your driver, make sure you hit down on the ball. If the ball is on the ground, you must hit down! If you don't hit down on the ball, you will probably hit the shot thin. If you hit the shot thin, the ball will probably not go over, but in.
- Use more club than you think you need because you would rather be long than short when going over trouble. You probably can play from long but possibly not from short.

When playing a round of golf, use more club than you think you need until proven wrong. If you think you need a 7-iron, use a 6-iron instead until you consistently go long.

If you are between clubs, take the shorter club if:

- There's trouble long.
- The front of the green is open.
- You are pumped up.

If you are between clubs, take the longer club if:

- There's trouble short.
- Your approach shots usually come up short.
- Your target is elevated.

As much as you can, try to keep the ball in the fairway. Keeping the ball in the fairway will give you more roll and should make your next shot easier.

From a good lie, use a 3-wood/metal. From a not-so-good lie, use a 5-wood/metal or 7-wood/metal. From a bad lie, use an iron.

The best way to play bunkers is to avoid them. If you cannot safely carry a bunker, lay up or go around it.

When your ball is in a bunker, your number one priority is to get your ball out of the bunker and back into play. See Chapter 14 and Chapter 15 for how to escape bunkers. Please note that I referred to this as to how to escape "bunkers" and not "traps." They say that traps are hard to get out of. I wouldn't know!

When your ball is in the rough, your number one goal is to get your ball out of the rough and back into play. See Chapter 12: Hitting Specialty Shots.

When you can putt, putt. When you can't putt, chip. When you can't chip, pitch. To learn all about putting, chipping, and pitching, see Chapter 16: The Short Game.

When putting, never concern yourself with the outcome of the putt because that is beyond your control. Some putts will mysteriously go in, and others will mysteriously stay out. The only thing you can control is your stroke. If you make a good stroke, more times than not, good things will happen.

If you are playing on greens that are not in the best condition, strike your putt firmly enough to hold its line. This is true on short putts as well.

If you are playing in a team format, such as the scramble format, remember that your putting line may be different from your partner's. The line you choose should always depend on the speed at which you roll your putts and not the speed others may roll theirs. This pointer is priceless!

Whether you are a beginner golfer or a seasoned pro, remember to have fun because golf is a game and games are created for fun. To better help you in your endeavor to have fun, check out Chapter 2: Mindset.

18
CHAPTER

HOW TO GET MORE DISTANCE

IN THE GOLF SWING, THERE ARE FOUR MAJOR SPEED PRODUCERS. SPEED PRODUCERS equal distance. Be sure to maximize all four of these major speed producers:

- The turn: The turn consists of the backswing, the downswing, and the follow-through. If you come up short on completing any of these three, your shots will forever come up short. In the backswing, the downswing, and the follow-through, the big muscles (shoulders, core, hips) are involved. Your shoulders, core, and hips will be involved if you keep your arms connected to your chest.

- The arms: When it comes to the arms, there are three key things to remember: First, the arms must stay connected to your chest. Second, the lead arm leads. For a right-handed golfer, the lead arm is the left arm. Third, during the swing, at least one arm must be fully extended at all times. From address to the start of your follow-through, your lead arm should be fully extended. Immediately after impact, both arms should be fully extended. From a little after impact to the finish, the trail arm should be fully extended. Having at least one arm fully extended at all times gives you a wide swing arc and allows your club to consistently come back to the same spot at impact.

- The hands: The hinging of the hands/wrists on the backswing, the unhinging of the hands/wrists at impact, and the rehinging of the hands/wrists on the follow-through is the number one speed producer in the golf swing. However, you should not consciously try to make this happen. It will happen naturally if you grip the club lightly enough to feel the weight of the clubhead. Consciously trying to make it happen will lead to inconsistent ball striking. Inconsistent ball striking is not what you want. See "Hands in the Golf Swing" in Chapter 6: The Golf Swing for detailed information regarding this.

- The clubface: To really pound the ball, you must hit the ball with the center of your clubface. If you are not hitting the ball with the center of your clubface, you are losing considerable distance (and accuracy) because you are hitting the ball with a glancing blow. To hit the ball with the center of your clubface, your clubface direction at impact and your swing path must match your target line. See "Grip Strength" in Chapter 3: Grip to refresh your memory on how to make this happen.

Additional Ways to Get More Distance:

- Hit down on the ball unless you are hitting your driver from a tee box.
- Have a slightly closed stance. This will have you swinging down from the inside, hitting a slight draw, which leads to more distance because you will get more roll.
- On the downswing, keep your lead shoulder closed or at least parallel to the target line through impact. This will allow you to hit the ball with everything you've got.
- Get your weight to the lead side on the downswing and follow-through. If you don't get your weight to the lead side on the downswing and follow-through, all the golf pointers in the world won't help you. (Thanks, SH!)
- Take a long club and use a long backswing because your distance is controlled by the length of your backswing.
- Swing through to the finish. If you don't swing through to the finish, you will probably not like where your ball finishes.
- On the downswing, pull the grip end of your club down with your lead arm as if you were jamming the butt of the club against an imaginary wall. Keep pulling the grip end of the club down all the way through the swing until the lead hand reaches hip-high on the follow-through. While pulling the grip end of the club down and through, turn your belt buckle toward the target. This will have you getting your weight to the lead side on the downswing and follow-through, have you getting your hands to the ball before the clubhead, and have you hitting the ball farther than you ever have. (Thanks, SC!)
- When you are pulling the grip end of your club down and through (previous thought), know that when the clubhead is going down, your hands are actually going up. This is what keeps you from bottoming out and puts the speed of your swing in the clubhead and not the grip end. These two moves combined will have you hitting shots off the chart. (Thanks, RTG!)
- Remember what you learned about the sledgehammer and scythe movement. See Chapter 6: The Golf Swing.

19

PRACTICE THOUGHTS AND DRILLS

THERE ARE PRACTICE THOUGHTS AND DRILLS SCATTERED THROUGHOUT THIS BOOK. When you come across a practice drill—don't just read about it—do it! Doing practice drills can improve your game overnight.

Before doing any practice drills, ensure that you have read Chapter 3: Grip and Chapter 4: Setup because in those two chapters, you will learn that your grip strength (strong, neutral, or weak) and your setup are inseparable. That fact can have more of an impact on your golf game than probably anything else in this book. By all means, check out those two chapters and do the two drills under "Grip Strength."

PRACTICING YOUR SHORT GAME

When it comes to practicing, all golf experts say that you should practice your short game first. Your short game consists of putting, chipping, and pitching. Your short game is discussed in great detail in Chapter 16: The Short Game. Please check out that chapter before proceeding with any of the following drills.

Practicing your short game first has many advantages. It is the quickest way to gain confidence and to take strokes off your game. It helps you to fully see the importance of your clubface direction and swing path. It helps you read greens. Reading greens well helps you immensely in understanding where to land your approach shots. To learn about approach shots, see "Approach Shot" in Chapter 12: Hitting Specialty Shots.

While the aforementioned reasons are important as to why to practice your short game first, probably the most important reason is that a full shot is just an extension of a chip shot. Learning to groove your swing on chip shots is a lot easier than trying to groove your swing on full shots. If you don't want to take the time to check out the entirety of Chapter 16: The Short Game, at least take the time to check out the "Chipping" segment. Understanding the chipping technique will take you a long way in developing a great golf swing.

A big part of the chipping technique goes as follows: On the downswing, swing your arms through the shot, keeping your lead wrist straight and firm—don't flip your wrists. At the end of your swing, the grip end of the club should point a little left of your lead hip and not back at your body. This is for right-handed golfers. It would be just the opposite for left-handed golfers.

Before hitting chip shots (or full shots), find a slight incline. Without a ball present, swing down into the side of the hill. Swing down into the side of the hill several times. This will give you the feeling of hitting down on the ball. Doing this drill each time before you hit chip or full shots will have you focusing on the spot you are attempting to hit and will keep you down on the ball. Both of these thoughts and feelings will serve you well on both chip and full shots.

Another great way to achieve the feeling of hitting down on the ball is to imagine you are starting your backswing from your impact position and not your address position. At your impact position, your hands would be ahead of the ball, your weight would be shifting to your lead side, and your lower body would be rotating toward the target. This will have you hitting down on the ball and will have you staying down on the ball. Two great things indeed!

Putting

For putting drills to do, please use Google because there are too many to list. However, in my opinion, the best putting drill you could ever do is going to any putting surface and practicing making putts. When you are practicing making these putts:

- Use three golf balls and select a shot.
- With the first ball, know the speed at which you intend to roll the ball and then select your line. Attempt to make the putt. See how you did.
- With the second ball, make whatever adjustments you need to make to the speed and/or line. Make the putt.
- With the third ball, make the putt again to show that making the second putt wasn't just luck.

When you first start out practicing your putting, you may want to start out with making two-foot uphill putts. By making these two-foot uphill practice putts, you will know that your putter face is square to your target line. Having your putter face square to your target line is 90 percent of the battle.

Another way to help keep your putter face square to your target line is to imagine a credit card under your ball and that it is square to your target line. Swing your putter face through the ball square to the credit card and target line.

If you are practicing your putting just before you play a round of golf, hit a few putts from one side of the practice green to the other without trying to sink a putt. Just putting from one side to the other will help you get the feel of the speed of the greens at that course that day.

On the practice green, also practice hitting lengthy putts with your trail hand only. Practicing lengthy putts, whether they go in or not, frees up your putting motion and keeps you from trying to steer the ball. If you try to steer the ball, you will tighten your muscles and you will usually just jab at the ball instead of making a good putting stroke. A good putting stroke is what you are after.

In addition to practicing lengthy putts, both uphill and downhill, practice making two- to four-foot putts. Practice making these two- to four-foot putts from all directions around the hole. During a round of golf, these short putts are the very putts that can make or break your round. When making these two- to four-foot putts, as with all putts, remember to make a stroke and not just jab at the ball.

On all putts, make a practice stroke first. This practice stroke will help you feel the length of the stroke you need for long putts and will help keep you from jabbing at the ball on short putts. Remember, on all shots, including putting, your distance is controlled by the length of your backswing.

Chipping

To practice your chipping, drop several balls ten feet or so from the green. Chip each of these balls toward the hole to see how much air and how much roll you get with each shot. See how your shots, using different clubs, compare to the "Rules of Thumb on Roll When Chipping," which you can find in Chapter 16: The Short Game.

When practicing, to help you determine the angle of your ball flight for a particular club, place the club on the ground with the clubface facing up and then step on the clubface. Your ball will come off at that angle.

Once you have determined how much air and how much roll you get with each club, hit ten to fifteen balls (or more) with the same club to home in your shot. This will go a long way in helping you determine which club to use for a particular shot when playing.

When practicing these chip shots, remember to swing your arms through the shot, keeping your lead wrist straight and firm—don't flip your wrists. At the end of your swing, the grip end of the club should point a little left of your lead hip and not back at your body. This is for right-handed golfers. It would be just the opposite for left-handed golfers.

Pitching

Drop several balls near obstacles that you must go over (water, ravine, or bunker) to see which club works best for you. When pitching, use a wedge or your 9-iron. When pitching, never use your sand wedge unless you have a soft and/or fluffy lie.

A great drill to practice your pitching is to attempt pitch shots using your trail hand only. Using just your trail hand when practicing pitch shots will keep you from having your hands too far forward, which delofts the club. On pitch shots, you want your hands even with or behind the ball, and you want to use the bounce of the club.

Another great drill for practicing your pitching is to have three different targets (clothes baskets, buckets, etc.). Your first target should be placed at twenty yards, your second target at forty yards, and your third target at sixty yards. Start out by attempting to hit your first target, the twenty-yard target. You don't necessarily have to ring the basket or bucket; you just want to hit the correct distance in the air. Once you have pretty much conquered that distance, shoot for the other targets. When shooting for these other targets, the only thing you want to do differently is to take a longer backswing because your distance is controlled by the length of your backswing.

PRACTICING THE REST OF YOUR GAME

In this segment, I will address the rest of your game—and I will try to address it in the order that you need it. Remember to study, practice, and then play!

Learn about Tempo and Rhythm

After working on your short game, the next thing you want to do is work on your tempo and rhythm with all your clubs. To learn about tempo and rhythm and to learn about a drill to do to improve your tempo and rhythm, see "Tempo and Rhythm" in Chapter 6: The Golf Swing.

Learn Your Natural Ball Flight

To learn your natural ball flight, pay attention to what your first five or six shots do when you are doing the first drill under "Grip Strength" in Chapter 3: Grip. If you are a right-handed golfer and your ball starts out to the left and then curves back to the right, you hit a natural fade. If you are a right-handed golfer and your ball starts out to the right and then curves back to the left, you hit a natural draw. It is good to know your natural ball flight so that up until the point you master hitting straight shots straight down your target line, you can fall back on your natural ball flight. To fall back on your natural ball flight, simply allow for and/or capitalize on it by changing your aiming point. Please take the time to do this drill.

Learn to Hit Fades and Draws

After learning to hit straight shots straight down your target line, learn to hit fades and draws. You can hit a fade or a draw by changing your grip or by changing your stance (setup). To change your grip, just undo what you did to hit the ball straight down your target line. To learn to hit fades and draws by changing your stance (setup), see Chapter 12: Hitting Specialty Shots. You want to learn to hit fades and draws, along with straight shots straight down your target line, because these three shots are the nucleus of your golf game.

Learn How Far You Hit Each Club

After doing all of the above, the next thing you want to do is learn how far you hit each club in the air. To learn how far you hit each club in the air, visit a driving range. Before visiting the driving range, check out Chapter 9: Club Selection.

Learn about Pre-Shot Routine

To learn about pre-shot routine, see Chapter 10: Pre-Shot Routine. All professional golfers have a pre-shot routine—you should have one as well. When hitting practice balls, you should use your pre-shot routine before every shot.

Hitting Your Driver

Take your shoe off of your trail foot (right foot for right-handed golfers). This will give you the feel of the proper weight distribution at address for hitting your driver.

Take a full backswing but, when you swing down and through, only hit the ball at approximately 20 percent of your speed. Then hit the ball at 40 percent, 60 percent, and finally at 80 percent. This will help you groove your swing by helping with your tempo and swing pattern.

To get more power with your driver, play the ball farther forward in your stance (about four to six inches farther forward than normal). Playing the ball farther forward when you practice will have you getting your weight to your lead side and will cause you to fully extend for the ball.

Hitting Fairway Woods/Metals

Full extension through the shot is the key to nailing your fairway woods/metals. Keep the clubhead low to the ground after impact and extend your arms and club shaft down the target line for as long as possible.

To make great contact with your fairway woods/metals, allow your arms to stretch out as you hit the shot. As your arms get longer, the club will make a wider arc, and the shaft will not lean severely behind the ball at impact. If the club shaft leans away from the target, you will lose power and distance.

When making practice swings with your fairway wood/metal, relax your arms and wrists. Feel the weight of the clubhead. As you do these practice swings, allow your arms to loosen up and make a wide arc when you swing the club down and through.

Hitting Hybrids

Hitting hybrids is more like hitting irons than woods/metals. Practice hitting hybrids correctly by hovering the clubhead a couple of inches off the ground at address. By hovering the clubhead off the ground, you'll instinctively hit down and through the ball to catch it solid.

Hitting Irons

Take your shoe off of your lead foot (left foot for right-handed golfers). This will give you the feel of the proper weight distribution at address for hitting irons.

Take a full backswing but, when you swing down and through, only hit the ball at approximately 20 percent of your speed. Then hit the ball at 40 percent, 60 percent, and finally at 80 percent. This will help you groove your swing by helping with your tempo and swing pattern.

When practicing hitting the long irons, you want to swing along the ground and not into the ground. To get the feel for how to do this, place a thin towel on the ground an inch behind the ball. Swing down so that you hit the ball but not the towel. The key to hitting the ball and not the towel is not in your hands and arms—it is in turning your big muscles (hips, core, shoulders) through the target and getting your weight to the lead side.

When hitting short irons and wedges, hit down on the ball. To help you get the feeling for hitting down on the ball, visualize having to hit your shot over a body of water. To make the ball go up and over, you must hit down with much vigor.

PRACTICING YOUR GAME USING PLASTIC BALLS

An excellent way to groove your golf swing and to get in a lot of practice time is to hit plastic balls (plastic balls with holes in them). The great thing about using plastic balls is that you can hit them almost anywhere—and you probably can hit them daily. What a great learning tool.

Another great thing about using plastic balls is that plastic balls will react to your swing in the exact same way as real golf balls. If you hit a slice with a golf ball, you will hit a slice with a plastic ball. If you hit the shot fat or thin with a golf ball, you will do the same with a plastic ball.

When hitting plastic balls, the balls are not going to go very far but that is okay. When hitting plastic balls, you are not working on your distance; you are working on your swing. (Thanks, LS!)

A great drill when hitting plastic balls is to take three of them and hit each one separately with your 7-iron. When hitting each of them take a full swing. Watch how each ball reacts. Did they go straight down your target line or did they go offline? If they went offline, revisit Chapter 5: Ball Flight Laws to understand why.

After you have hit each of them, go up and hit each of them again as if you were chipping them up onto a green. When chipping these balls up onto an imaginary green, remember what you learned in Chapter 16: The Short Game. This drill will help you immensely in getting the feel for hitting straight shots and creating muscle memory. Hitting straight shots and creating good muscle memory are two powerful and desirable things.

In addition to hitting these plastic balls with your 7-iron, I would strongly suggest that you practice hitting these plastic balls with your wedges to make pitch shots. This exercise will lead to confidence when making pitch shots on the course.

ADDITIONAL THOUGHTS REGARDING PRACTICING

- When you practice, video your swing on each type of shot, including putting, chipping, and pitching—so that you can see what you are doing during your swing. A lot of times what we are actually doing is a lot different from what we think we are doing.

- When you practice, work on your swing. When you play, work on your game.

- In a round of golf, most golfers only use their driver fourteen times, so—instead of spending the majority of your practice time hitting your driver, why not practice hitting the clubs you use the most? Tracking how far you hit each club in the air should give you a good indication as to which clubs you use the most.

- To hit great shots, proper alignment is vital. If you don't line up properly, you can have the most beautiful golf swing in the world, yet you will still struggle with your golf game. See "Alignment" in Chapter 4: Setup.

- For proper alignment, when practicing, place a club or an alignment stick on the ground just outside the ball parallel to the target line. Then place another club or alignment stick on the ground closer to your feet parallel to that line. Have your shoulders, hips, knees, and feet parallel to the target line. Of these four, the shoulders are the most important because you will always swing along your shoulder line.

- To ensure that your clubface is square to the ball and target line at address and impact, when you practice, square your clubface up to an empty box—this will let you know what square looks like to you with each club at the address position.

- To help you turn on your backswing—and avoid swaying, place a wooden wedge under the outside of your trail heel. This will force your weight to remain on the inside of your trail foot, which is where it should be on your backswing.

- To get your weight to the lead side on the downswing, imagine you are hitting a forehand in tennis. When hitting a forehand in tennis, you would never keep your weight on the trail side. When hitting a golf shot, you shouldn't either.

- To further help you get your weight to the lead side, play the ball five to six inches farther forward in your stance than you normally would. This will have you getting your weight to the lead side and will have you swinging all the way through the ball and not just to the ball.

- To get the feel for using your big muscles (shoulders, core, hips) and keeping your arms connected to your chest during the swing, extend a golf towel across your chest, and hold it in place under your arms while doing the following drill. Place your ball on a low tee. Use your 7-iron and hit three-quarter shots keeping the towel under your arms. Notice how the towel makes you turn your body in sync with your arms. Also, notice that the balls you are hitting have a slight draw, which is a good thing—unless you are trying to hit a fade.

- To get the correct feel of feeling the weight of the clubhead, make practice swings with your 3-wood/metal. Feel how the weight of the clubhead makes your arms get long. Long arms equal long shots. For more power and distance, get this feel with all of your clubs. Note: If you cannot feel the weight of the clubhead, you are gripping the club too tightly.

- To get the speed at the correct point in your swing, turn the club upside down and grip it near the hosel. Make a few practice swings and make sure the "swoosh" sound is loudest just in front of where the ball should be (target side).

- To get the feel of having your hands get to the ball first, hit delofted shots using lofted clubs (short irons or wedges). The only way to do that is to have your hands ahead of the ball at the point of impact.

- To get the proper feel for when to release the club, sling old clubs down the target line. When doing this drill, ensure that you sling the club straight down your target line.

- To develop a consistent golf swing, tee the ball low and use your 7-iron. On the downswing, clip the tee each time. This will eliminate you hitting fat shots (hitting the ground first) and thin shots (hitting the upper half of the ball).

- A drill to keep the correct angle with your trail leg is to lift your lead heel off the ground so that your weight is on your trail leg as you are in your stance. With the heel of your lead foot off the ground, you will have to stay in your stance. Only use this drill when practicing because when you are playing, you want to get your weight to the lead side on the downswing and follow-through. You can't do this if you have your lead heel off the ground.

- To ensure that your weight is on your lead foot when hitting approach shots, lift the heel of your trail foot about half an inch and hit down on the ball.

- Make practice swings before making the shot. When making practice swings, note where the club brushes the ground on the downswing. With all clubs other than your driver and putter, play the ball just back of that spot so that you can make ball-first contact. With all clubs other than your driver and putter, hit down on the ball, hitting ball first and then taking a divot on the target side of the ball. When you are hitting down on the ball, the hands are actually going up while the clubhead is going down.

- When making practice swings, pay attention to the depth of your swing. Make sure that you get the depth right for the club that you are using and the shot that you are attempting to make. With the long clubs, you want to sweep the ball off the turf if the ball is sitting up nicely. In this case, you wouldn't take much of a divot. With the long clubs, if the ball is not sitting up nicely, you want to take a slight divot on the target side of the ball. With the mid irons, you want to hit down on the ball just a little taking a long, shallow divot on the target side of the ball. With the short irons and wedges, you want to hit down on the ball, taking a fairly good-sized divot on the target side of the ball. With the short irons and wedges, if you want the ball to go up, you must hit down!

- When making practice swings, focus on your finish. To achieve a good finish position, your belt buckle should point at, or slightly left of, the target (for right-handed golfers). Your eyes should be looking down the fairway, and 90 percent of your weight should be over your lead foot. On full shots, the club should be wrapped around your lead shoulder.

- To get the feel for how to hit your driver, throw a bale of hay onto a low trailer. If you can't get your hands on a bale of hay, or if a bale of hay is simply too heavy for you, use a bale of pine straw instead. This motion will let you know how important it is to have a solid foundation and will also demonstrate how the weight of the bale will pull you back to the inside on the backswing and pull you through on the downswing. Feeling the weight of the clubhead when you swing a golf club should give you this same sensation.

- A great way to improve your game while practicing is to visualize playing a round of golf. Practice hitting the tee shot that you would need to hit on the first hole of the course you normally play or the course that you are about to play. Practice hitting the second shot that you would normally have to hit on that hole. Continue this format until you have played the full eighteen holes. You will be amazed at how much this helps you in lowering your score when you play that course.

- The best way to improve your game is by practicing, and the best way to practice is to play the majority of your rounds as practice rounds. When playing these practice rounds, don't worry about keeping score because at this time you are not working on your score, you are working on your game.

- When playing these practice rounds, if you are not holding anyone up, hit more than one shot from each lie. This way, you can improve on each swing and fully determine for future reference which is the correct club for that distance and lie. If you would be holding someone up by hitting more than one shot, simply step aside and let them play through. That way you can truly work on your game while allowing them to enjoy their game. Definitely a win-win for everyone! I am amazed at the number of golfers who never play practice rounds. Instead, they always play as if they are in a tournament. They hit one shot from each lie and then they move on to their next shot from usually an altogether different lie. From each area, they hit a somewhat good shot or a terrible shot. Either way, they move on, never knowing if that was truly the best club and best shot from that lie and distance. Amateur golfers do this and wonder why their golf game never improves. I guarantee you that if the pros did it this way, they wouldn't be pros for very long.

- Another great practice format is to hit two balls each time and play the best ball. This will give you an opportunity to figure out what you did wrong on the first shot and immediately correct it. This format will give you an idea about what your game could be.

- In keeping with that concept, the next time you play a practice round, hit two balls each time but this time play the worst ball. This will give you an opportunity to hit shots from all different kinds of locations. This format will go a long way in helping you build confidence in your scoring ability because you will learn that you can make a good golf shot from almost anywhere. Under this format, instead of cursing where your ball went, you could think, "Hey, I have never had the opportunity to hit a ball from this location or lie. This could be kind of cool." Once you make the shot, you will feel even cooler! In fact, your friends might even say, "Hey, is that ice falling off of you?" (I'm just saying.)

20
<u>CHAPTER</u>

FAULTS AND FIXES

WHEN IT COMES TO FAULTS AND FIXES, PLEASE REALIZE THAT THERE IS USUALLY MORE than one fix for your fault. My suggestion is to try them all, one at a time, until you come up with the fix that works best for your fault. If you try too many fixes at the same time, you are probably going to do more harm than good because even if you fix the fault, you won't be able to tell which one was the best fix.

Before digging into the information in this chapter, I encourage you to check out and/or review Chapter 5: Ball Flight Laws. Be sure to check out the "Ball Flight Laws Diagram" and the explanations for why the ball goes where it goes. It is better to learn how to do it right in the first place than trying to learn how to fix it later!

In addition, before digging into the information in this chapter, review the information under "Grip Strength" in Chapter 3: Grip. If you haven't done the two drills suggested there, please take the time to do them. Taking the time to do them may very well cure your faults.

Fault: The Slice
The slice is probably the #1 fault in golf. According to the golfing experts, 80 percent of amateur golfers slice the ball. With a slice, the ball starts out to the left of the target and then curves back to the right, for right-handed golfers, usually way off target. For left-handed golfers, the ball starts out to the right and then curves back to the left, again, usually way off target. With this shot, you lose both accuracy and distance.

<u>Fix</u>
To fix the slice, do the following:

- Try a stronger grip. A stronger grip can help eliminate a slice and can possibly even have you slightly drawing the ball. See "Grip Strength" in Chapter 3: Grip.
- Stop aiming left if you are a right-handed golfer. Stop aiming right if you are a left-handed golfer. Set up parallel to the target line—or set up with a slightly closed stance—and swing down the target line. If you are a right-handed golfer and you aim farther left, you are going to slice even more. If you are a left-handed golfer and you aim farther right, you are going to slice even more.
- Play the ball in the correct position in your stance. If you play the ball too far forward in your stance, by the time your clubface gets to the ball, the clubface will be open to your swing path, which leads to a slice. See "Ball Position" in Chapter 4: Setup for guidelines on correct ball position.
- Stand closer to the ball. Standing too far from the ball pulls the upper body downward, leading to a compensating stand-up move through impact. This standing up motion usually leads to a slice. To ensure that you are standing the correct distance from the ball, once you have set up in your stance, take your trail hand off of your club. Your trail arm should hang straight down beside your lead arm. If it does not, you are standing too close to the ball or too far away from the ball.
- On the backswing, turn your back to the target before raising the clubhead. Turning your back to the target will bring the club inside.
- On the downswing, swing down from the inside, in-to-square-to-in. To swing down from the inside, your clubhead can never get outside your target line. To swing down from the inside, your hands must be closer to the target line than your clubhead until impact.
- On the downswing, drop your arms straight down behind you while turning your lower body (knees and hips) toward the target. If you drop your arms down toward the ball instead of behind you, your arms and hands will take over the swing and you will be swinging outside-in, which will lead to a pull or a slice, depending on which way the clubface is pointing at impact. (See Chapter 5: Ball Flight Laws.)
- On the downswing, remember the sledgehammer and scythe movements discussed in Chapter 6: The Golf Swing.
- On the downswing, pull the grip end of your club down with your lead arm as if you were jamming the butt of the club against an imaginary wall. Keep pulling the grip end of the club down all the way through the swing until the lead hand reaches hip-high on the follow-through. While pulling the grip end of the club down and through, turn your belt buckle toward the target. This will have you getting your weight to the lead side on the downswing and follow-through, have

you getting your hands to the ball before the clubhead, and have you hitting the ball farther than you ever have. (Thanks, SC!)

- When you are pulling the grip end of your club down and through (previous thought), know that when the clubhead is going down, your hands are actually going up. This is what keeps you from bottoming out and is what puts the speed of your swing in the clubhead and not the grip end. These two moves combined will have you hitting the ball straight down your target line and will have you hitting balls off the chart. (Thanks, RTG!)
- A slice and a pull are both produced by the same type of downswing, an outside-in swing. The only difference between these two shots is the direction that the clubface is pointing at impact. On a slice, you swing from outside-in with the clubface open to your swing path. On a pull, you swing from outside-in with the clubface square to your swing path. To fix both the slice and the pull, start the ball to the right of your target (for right-handed golfers). Do this by pulling your trail foot back from the target line at address. This will have you attacking the ball from the inside, giving your swing a nice, rounded quality.

Fault: The Push

With a push, the golf ball starts right of your target (for right-handed golfers) and continues in that direction. A push can be caused by playing the ball too far back in your stance, by swinging inside-out, or by not finishing your swing.

Fix

To fix a push, play the ball in the correct position in your stance, ensure that you swing along the proper line, and finish your swing. See "Ball Position" in Chapter 4: Setup for correct ball position. To ensure you swing along the proper line, remember that for straight shots straight down your target line, on the downswing, you want to swing down from the inside, in-to-square-to-in. To ensure that you swing through to the finish, revisit "Finish" in Chapter 7: The Golf Swing (Broken Down).

Fault: Hitting the Shot Fat or Thin

Hitting the shot fat or thin is caused by the same fault, which is failing to get your weight to the lead side on the downswing and follow-through. You hit the ball fat when your club bottoms out before the ball. You hit the ball thin when your club has already bottomed out behind your ball and is on the way up when it strikes the ball, catching the top half of the ball.

Fix

To avoid hitting fat and/or thin shots:

- Play the ball in the correct position in your stance.
- Swing on plane. To swing on plane, visualize swinging along a slanted, glass tabletop, with the tabletop slanted at the same angle as your club shaft at address. With the long clubs, your swing plane will be more horizontal. With the short irons and wedges, your swing plane will be more vertical. Folding your trail arm at the elbow on the backswing, while hinging your wrists, and folding your lead arm at the elbow on the follow-through, while rehinging your wrists, is what allows you to swing on plane.
- Stay down on the ball. Your chest should stay the same distance from the ground from address to impact. Remember, you swing around your spine. Your chest is just in front of your spine.
- Maintain the same spine angle from address to impact by maintaining the same amount of flex in your trail leg from address to impact. If you tend to raise up in your backswing, you may want to consider just going ahead and starting in that position at address.
- Hit the face of the ball with the face of the club no matter which club you are using unless you are making a greenside bunker shot. Use the club that will allow you to hit the face of the ball and then worry about your needed distance. (For additional vigor in your swing, imagine that you are hitting the face of someone you do not particularly care for!)
- With all clubs other than your driver (and putter), hit down on the ball. When hitting down on the ball, hit the ball first, and then the ground.
- Make sure you take a divot on the target side of the ball. If you hit the ball only instead of the ball first and then the ground, there is a good chance that your clubhead has already started coming up. If your clubhead is coming up, you will hit the ball thin.
- On the downswing and follow-through, get 90 percent of your weight to the lead side. Your swing will always bottom out where your weight is. If the spot where your swing bottoms out is inconsistent, so will be your shots.
- Ensure that your hands and arms don't outrace your body to the ball. Your hands and arms will outrace your body if you stop turning your body toward the target on the downswing. When turning your body toward the target, you want to turn in the following sequence: lead knee, belt buckle, upper body, arms, and then the clubhead.
- Ensure that your downswing is not too much inside-out; you want to swing down from the inside, in-to-square-to-in.

Fault: Trying to Pick the Ball Clean

If you try to pick the ball clean, rather than hitting down on it, you will probably forever struggle with your golf game. When you attempt to pick the ball clean, you may sometimes hit a beautiful shot. However, you will probably come to find that, just as often, you hit the ground behind the ball or only hit the ball a third of the needed distance. It is hard to make consistent contact when you are trying to pick the ball clean. The only time you want to pick the ball clean is when you are making a shot from a fairway bunker.

Fix

Instead of trying to pick the ball clean, hit down on the ball. With all clubs, other than your driver and putter, you should hit down on the ball. When hitting down on the ball, the hands are actually going up while the clubhead is going down.

With the long clubs, you want to hit just slightly down on the ball and take a slight divot on the target side of the ball. With the short irons and wedges, you want to hit down on the ball pretty drastically and take a fairly good-sized divot on the target side of the ball.

When taking a divot, your divot should be on the target side of the ball. To get the feel for this, when practicing, draw a horizontal line in the center of your stance. Draw this line for about two feet directly in front of you at a ninety-degree angle to your shoulder line. Now, make practice swings without a ball being present, ensuring that you take a divot each time. This divot should start on the line and go toward the imaginary target. Do this drill with all of your irons, including your wedges. This drill will have you hitting down on the ball rather than trying to pick the ball clean.

Fault: Spinning Out During the Downswing

In an effort to hit the ball farther, beginners and somewhat struggling golfers often attempt to hit the ball harder. When these golfers attempt to hit the ball harder, they usually spin out during the downswing and then there is no telling where their ball is going to go. Instead of trying to hit the ball harder, in actuality, they should be trying to hit the ball farther.

Fix

To hit the ball farther, simply take a long club and use a long backswing because your distance is controlled by the length of your backswing, which includes the length of your club. In addition, swing through to the finish. If you don't swing through to the finish, you will probably not like where your ball finishes.

To help keep you from spinning out during the downswing, keep your lead shoulder closed or at least parallel to the target line for as long as you can on the downswing. This one move alone will do wonders in having you pounding the ball down the center of your target line.

Fault: Losing Your Balance During the Swing
If you are consistently losing your balance during your swing, either you are overswinging or your stance is too narrow. Pay attention to both your swing effort and your stance-width to determine which one is the culprit.

<u>Fix</u>
If you are overswinging, see the fix regarding spinning out during the downswing. If your stance is too narrow, see the following. For the mid irons (5-, 6-, 7-iron), the insides of your feet should be shoulder-width apart. The stance for the long irons and woods should be two inches wider. The stance for the short irons should be two inches narrower.

Fault: Getting When You Push and When You Pull Mixed Up
Most amateur golfers pull when they should push and push when they should pull.

<u>Fix</u>
You push on the backswing and pull on the downswing. On the backswing, push the club back with your lead shoulder and lead arm. On the downswing, pull the grip end of the club down with your lead arm as if you were jamming the butt of the club against an imaginary wall. Keep pulling the grip end of the club down all the way through the swing until the lead hand reaches hip-high on the follow-through. While pulling the grip end of the club down and through, turn your belt buckle toward the target. This will have you getting your weight to the lead side on the downswing and follow-through, have you getting your hands to the ball before the clubhead, and have you hitting the ball farther than you ever have. (Thanks, SC!)

When you are pulling the grip end of your club down and through (previous thought), know that when the clubhead is going down, your hands are actually going up. This is what keeps you from bottoming out and is what puts the speed of your swing in the clubhead, not the grip end. These two moves combined will have you hitting shots off of the chart. (Thanks, RTG!)

Fault: Pulling Your Short Irons and Wedges

A lot of golfers pull their short irons and wedges. The three main reasons for this are that they swing outside-in, they play their ball too far forward, or they start their downswing with their lower body (knees and hips).

Fix

To fix this problem, you need to check out all three of these reasons to see which one is the culprit. To check to see whether it is your swing path, revisit the second drill under "Grip Strength" in Chapter 3: Grip. To check to see whether you are playing the ball too far forward in your stance, revisit "Ball Position" in Chapter 4: Setup. To fix the last fault, know that with the short irons and wedges, the clubhead initiates the downswing and not the lower body. With the short irons and wedges, if you start the downswing with your lower body, you will swing outside-in, pulling the ball.

Fault: Coming up Short

In golf, you should never come up short on any shot, because any time you come up short, it will cost you at least one more stroke. (Thanks, TK!)

Fix

When playing a round of golf, use more club than you think you need until proven wrong. If you think you need a 7-iron, use a 6-iron instead. You should be able to hit a 6-iron ten yards farther than a 7-iron. Continue doing this until you consistently don't come up short.

When hitting approach shots, chip shots, and pitch shots, don't come up short. When putting, make sure that you don't come up short because you miss 100 percent of those putts. With all putts, you should stroke the ball firmly enough that the ball will roll 18 inches past the hole if it doesn't go in. Having that thought in mind goes a long way toward helping you get your putts to the hole.

Additional Faults and Fixes

At address, never extend your arms and reach for the ball. Your arms should hang straight down and relaxed from your shoulder sockets. Your hands should hang over your toe line. At address, you should be looking in at your hands and not out at them. To ensure that you are not reaching for the ball, set up to the ball and then take your trail hand off the club. Your trail hand should hang naturally down right beside your lead hand which should still be on the club.

If you play the ball too far back in your stance, you will deloft your club and hit low shots even when you may not want to. To hit the ball high, play the ball a little farther forward in your stance. Start with high hands (on your backswing) and finish with high hands (on the follow-through).

Remember, you can add loft to any club by opening your stance a bit. If you open your stance a bit, aim a little farther left (for right-handed golfers) because the ball will tend to go a little right. Left-handed golfers should do the exact opposite.

Push the club back with your lead shoulder—and don't pull back with your trail hand. Pushing back with your lead shoulder keeps the arms connected to the chest and has the club going back on the correct path.

Don't swing too horizontally because a horizontal swing produces slices and pulls. If you are short in stature, your swing will be more horizontal than that of a taller golfer—but keep your swing as vertical as you can while maintaining your spine angle.

At impact, ensure that the grip end of your club shaft does not lean away from the target, unless you are hitting your driver; otherwise, you will lose power and distance. At impact, with all clubs other than your driver, the grip end of your club shaft should be leaning slightly toward the target. The more consistent this lean, the more consistent your shots will be. With your driver, your club shaft should be leaning away from the target at impact because you play your ball the most forward in your stance, the ball is teed up, and you want to hit the ball on the upswing.

To avoid hitting the ball off the hosel, ensure that the leading edge of the club is level when it comes into the ball. Ensure that the heel of the club is not off the ground.

To ensure that you are making the correct swing, check your divots. Your divots should be past the ball (target side) and not before the ball.

If your swing is too steep (vertical), practice hitting shots that are above your feet. This will get you swinging more horizontally.

If your swing is too flat (horizontal), practice hitting shots that are below your feet. This will get you swinging more vertically.

When putting, if you lift your body on the backswing, you will push the ball. If you open your lead shoulder on the downswing, you will pull the ball. If you don't hit the ball in the center of your clubface (putter face), you will lose distance and direction.

21
<u>CHAPTER</u>

QUICK POINTERS

THE POINTERS IN THIS CHAPTER ARE PUT HERE FOR THOSE WHO NEED TO PLAY A round of golf before they have time to read this book in the order in which it is laid out. While starting with this chapter is not the best way to go about learning how to play and excel at golf, hopefully the information in this chapter will be enough to allow you an enjoyable round of golf. Please read the entirety of this chapter before proceeding!

In addition to checking out this chapter, please check out Chapter 22: Golf Etiquette. The thoughts and pointers in that chapter, if adhered to, should be more than enough to allow everyone around you the opportunity for an enjoyable round of golf.

Your ball flight is determined by your clubface direction at impact (85%) and by your swing path (15%). Your clubface direction is determined by your grip strength (strong, neutral, or weak). Your swing path is greatly influenced by your setup because you will always swing along your shoulder line.

With the information above in mind, the first thing you want to do is learn to hit straight shots. The second thing you want to do is learn to hit these straight shots straight down your target line. The third thing you want to do is learn your natural ball flight. To learn these three things, do the first drill under "Grip Strength" in Chapter 3: Grip.

If you are a beginner golfer, read Chapter 3: Grip in its entirety. To further help you learn to hit straight shots straight down your target line, see Chapter 4: Setup and Chapter 8: Drawings.

To learn your natural ball flight, simply pay attention to what your first five or six shots do when you are doing the first drill under "Grip Strength" in Chapter 3: Grip. If you are a right-handed golfer and your first five or six shots start out left and then curve back to the right, you hit a natural fade. If you are a right-handed golfer and your first five or six shots start out right and then curve back to the left, you hit a natural draw. If you are a left-handed golfer, it would be just the opposite.

Knowing your natural ball flight can really help your game, especially if you are a beginner golfer. Until you master the art of hitting straight shots straight down your target line, you may want to play your natural ball flight as often as you can. If you are a right-handed golfer and you hit a natural fade, rather than aiming straight down the target line, aim a little left and let the ball curve back to the target. If you are a right-handed golfer and you hit a natural draw, rather than aiming straight down the target line, aim a little right and let the ball curve back to the target. If you are a left-handed golfer, do the exact opposite.

To learn how to hit fades and draws, as well as straight shots straight down your target line, see Chapter 12: Hitting Specialty Shots. You want to learn how to hit these three shots because they are the nucleus of your golf game.

After reading about how to hit these three shots, check out Chapter 13: Hitting from Uneven Lies because every uneven lie has its own ball flight tendency. The better you know these ball flight tendencies, the better your results will be.

Next, check out Chapter 9: Club Selection and Chapter 10: Pre-Shot Routine. In Chapter 9, you will learn all about the different clubs. In Chapter 10, you will learn how to decide which club to use for each shot. Knowing this information can have a great impact on your game.

If you have any time left before your golf outing, check out:

- Chapter 5: Ball Flight Laws
- Chapter 6: The Golf Swing
- Chapter 14: Hitting from Fairway Bunkers
- Chapter 15: Hitting from Greenside Bunkers
- Chapter 16: The Short Game
- Chapter 17: Golf Wisdom

Additional Pointers

Golf is a lot like bowling. If you grip it correctly, aim correctly, and sling (swing) it correctly, good things are usually going to happen.

The feet are the foundation of the swing. The spine is the axis of the swing. The lead hand is the fulcrum of the swing.

Turn on the backswing—don't sway. If you sway on the backswing, there is no way that you can consistently return to the same spot on the downswing.

On the downswing, get your weight to the lead side. If you don't get your weight to the lead side on the downswing and follow-through, all the golf pointers in the world won't help you. (Thanks, SH!)

On the downswing, instead of trying to add speed to the clubhead with your hands, swing the grip end of the club and let the clubhead take care of itself. Centrifugal force will provide the speed and square the clubhead.

Swing through to the finish. If you don't swing through to the finish, you will probably not like where your ball finishes.

Hope these pointers are helpful. Good luck and may the course be with you!

22
CHAPTER

GOLF ETIQUETTE

Please check out the following suggestions and please feel free to add any that you may think will speed up the game and will make it more enjoyable for everyone. Remember, golf etiquette is everybody's business because we all want to play on nice courses and we all want the game to move fluidly.

Suggestions to consider:

- Be ready to play when it is your turn. That means already having your club in hand, if feasible, and having a general idea about what kind of shot you are going to make.
- When it is your turn, please stop talking and hit the ball. You can finish your story when you get back in the golf cart or in the club house.
- Please be quiet when others are about to play.
- Fix your divots after each shot.
- After hitting from a bunker, please rake the bunker. When you have finished raking the bunker, place the rake in a position where it will not interfere with future play.
- Please repair ball marks on the green—and ask for help if you need to be shown the correct technique.
- On the green, don't walk on others' putting line.
- When walking on the green, pick up your feet to lessen damage to the turf.
- Don't hit into the group ahead of you. If you are playing faster than they are, hopefully they know about golf etiquette and will allow you to play through.
- If the group behind you is playing faster, please let them play through. Letting them play through will not cost you much time and it will make for a much more

enjoyable round for everyone. Usually a par 3 is the best time to let someone play through.

- When riding from shot to shot, attempt to stay off the fairway as much as possible.
- During wet conditions on the course, please adhere to the ninety-degree rule. The ninety-degree rule means driving down the edge of the fairway and then turning at a ninety-degree angle to head straight for your ball. If the conditions are extremely wet, please don't drive the cart onto the fairway at all because it can really tear up the ground.
- Don't write down your score until you are at the next tee box. This will speed up the game for you and the group behind you.
- After the completion of your round, please clear the green as quickly as reasonably possible. This will speed up the game for the group behind you.

Not only do I thank you for doing your part but the entire golfing community applauds you. Great job!

23
<u>CHAPTER</u>

CLOSING COMMENTS

THANK YOU FOR TAKING THE TIME TO READ THIS BOOK. I HOPE IT HAS BEEN HELPFUL.

For those of you who really want to take your game to the next level, I strongly recommend reading and rereading this book, or your "mini-book," as many times as it takes. Don't forget, the more you put in, the more you get out. Also, remember that you read to learn and you take notes to remember.

In addition to reading and studying this book, please take the time to practice. Doing practice drills correctly can improve your game overnight. Remember, the cool thing about golf is that you can practice it for hours on end or for ten to fifteen minutes at a time. Also remember, when it comes to practicing, the biggest difference between great golfers and struggling golfers is that great golfers practice the things they are not so good at and struggling golfers practice the things they are good at. If you want to be a great, or somewhat improved golfer (and who doesn't?), practice the things that you are not so good at.

When studying, practicing, and playing the game of golf, I sincerely hope that you will adopt the correct mindset because it is your mindset that separates you from all other golfers. For ideas on how to adopt the correct mindset, revisit Chapter 2: Mindset.

In addition to working on your own game, I hope that you will take this recently acquired knowledge and skill and share it with others. Perhaps you could share it with the youth in your community or someone who may be a little less fortunate than yourself? By sharing the game with others, you would not only be growing the game but you would be growing the love between you and your fellowman. Just think what an impact we could make on the world if each and every one of us did this. What an awesome opportunity!

Remember, if you want to make a difference in the world, make a difference in yourself!

With much love,

Ron Strickland

GLOSSARY

A

A-game: The best a golfer can play, as in, "You'd better bring your A-game."

ace: Hole-in-one. (Every golfer's ultimate goal.)

address: The position a player gets into as they prepare to make a swing.

air ball: When your swing misses the ball. (Once you start keeping score for real, it counts as a stroke because you took a swing attempting to advance the ball.)

albatross: British term for *double eagle* (which is three under par on one hole).

alignment: Refers to body position prior to the swing. For a straight shot straight down your target line, if your shoulders, hips, knees, and feet are parallel to your target line, you are in proper alignment.

approach shot: Shot that is expected to reach the green.

apron: The grass around the edge of a green, which is longer than the grass on the green but shorter than the grass on the fairway. Also called the *fringe* or *collar*.

attend: To hold and remove the flagstick as another player putts.

away: Term used to describe the ball lying farthest from the hole and, therefore, next to be played.

axis: Refers to the spine, which is the center of the swing motion and is what the body swings around.

B

back nine: The second half of your round of golf, usually holes 10 through 18.

backspin: A backward spinning motion of the ball.

bail out: When you hit the shot to one side or another to avoid trouble on the other side.

balance: To make a good swing, you must swing and finish in balance.

ball marker: A small, flat object used to indicate the ball's position on the green.

ball retriever: A telescoping pole with a cup on the end used to collect balls from water hazards, ravines, woods, etc.

ball washer: A device for cleaning balls, usually found near some tee boxes and on driving ranges.

banana ball: A shot that curves sharply from left to right (for right-handed golfers)—a slice.

baseball grip: Also called *ten-finger grip*. Type of grip where all ten fingers are on the club. Sometimes used by individuals with small hands.

best ball: A game in which two or more players form a team. Each player plays his or her own ball, and only the best score from each team is recorded. Don't confuse *best ball* with the *select-a-shot* and/or *scramble* format.

birdie: A score of one stroke under par on a hole.

bite: A spin that makes the ball stop rather than roll when it lands.

blade: A forged iron clubhead that offers superior feel at impact but is less forgiving to off-center strikes. *Blade* also refers to the leading edge of an iron.

bogey: A score of one stroke over par on a hole.

bounce: The wide flange on the sole of a sand wedge.

break: The amount of curve you must allow for a putt on a sloping green.

bump-and-run: A type of chip shot that is in the air for only a short time and then rolls the rest of the way—this is the safest chip shot you can make—and is often done with a 7-iron.

bunker: A hazard filled with sand. (Refrain from referring to bunkers as *sand traps* because the word *trap* insinuates that you can't get out.)

buried lie: A lie where part of the ball is below the surface of the sand in a bunker. Also referred to as a *fried egg*.

C

caddie: The person who carries a golfer's clubs during a round of golf if the golfer is not carrying the clubs himself/herself.

carry: The distance a ball flies through the air.

casting: Early release of the club during the downswing, which can lead to the lead wrist being cupped at impact. This leads to a weak shot with a lot of spin on the ball.

casual water: Water other than a water hazard on the course, such as a puddle, from which you can lift your ball without penalty.

cavity back: An iron with the back of the head hollowed out, which positions weight around the perimeter of the clubhead. This increases the mass behind off-center strikes, which makes it a more forgiving club.

center-shafted: A putter in which the shaft is connected to the center of the head.

chip: A low shot that travels farther on the ground than it does in the air. It is frequently used to get a ball onto the green when there is no trouble between the ball and the green.

chip-in: A holed chip.

choke: To play poorly because of self-imposed pressure. Also, a term to never be used around a game of sports. Rather than "choke down" on a club, you want to "grip down" on a club.

closed clubface: Clubface pointed to the left of your target at address or impact (for right-handed golfers).

closed stance: An address position in which the golfer's alignment is to the right of the target (for right-handed golfers).

clubface: The front, flat portion of the club that is designed to contact the ball.

clubhead: The end portion of a golf club that is designed to hit the ball.

club length: The distance from the end of the grip to the bottom of the clubhead.

collar: See *apron*.

cup: Container in the hole that holds the flagstick in place.

cut shot: Shot that curves from left to right (for right-handed golfers).

D

dance floor: Another name for the green.

deloft the club: You deloft the club by leaning the club shaft forward toward the target. You should do this on most, but not all, shots. When you do need to deloft the club, do it just before you start your backswing.

divot: A piece of turf that has been torn from the ground by a golf swing.

divot mark: The hole in the ground from where a divot was taken.

dogleg: A hole on which the fairway curves sharply one way or the other.

double bogey: A score of two strokes over par on a hole.

double eagle: A score of three strokes under par on a hole.

downhill lie: When your trail foot (right foot for right-handed golfers) is higher than your lead foot at address.

downswing: The part of the swing where the clubhead is moving down toward the ball.

draw: Shot that moves, subtly, on a right-to-left trajectory (for right-handed golfers) due to sidespin imparted by the direction the clubface was pointing at impact.

drive: Shot from a tee box using your driver.

drive the green: When your drive finishes on the putting surface.

driver: The club that has the least amount of loft, other than the putter. This club is also the longest club in the bag and is expected to hit the ball the farthest. This club is normally used to hit a ball off a tee on a par-4 and a par-5.

driving range: A designated place where you can go to hit practice balls.

drop: Procedure by which you put a ball back into play after it has been lifted and/or replaced in accordance with one of the rules of golf.

duck hook: A shot curving severely from right to left (for right-handed golfers).

E

eagle: A score of two strokes under par for a hole.

etiquette: How you should conduct yourself on the course (see Chapter 22: Golf Etiquette).

F

face: The front of a clubhead or bunker.

fade: Shot that curves gently from left to right (for right-handed golfers) due to sidespin imparted at impact.

fairway: The closely mowed turf running from tee to green.

fairway wood: Similar in shape, but slightly smaller than the driver. This club has more loft than the driver and can hit the ball a long way from the fairway or from the tee. When hitting a fairway wood off a tee, tee the ball up lower than with a driver.

fat shot: When you hit the ground before the ball on the downswing. The turf gets stuck between the clubface and the ball, costing you a lot of distance.

first cut: Strip of rough at the edge of the fairway.

flag: Piece of cloth attached to the top of a flagstick.

flagstick: The pole with the flag on top, which indicates where the cup is. Also called the *pin*.

flange: Projecting piece of clubhead behind the sole.

flex: The amount of bend (flexibility) in a club shaft (see your golf pro and/or golf vendor). Also, the amount of bend in your knees at address and during the swing.

flier: Shot hit from the rough that travels farther than usual.

follow-through: The part of the swing immediately after the ball has been struck.

fore: What to shout when your ball is headed toward another person.

forged irons: Clubs made by hand.

forward press: Shifting the hands forward, toward the target, just before you begin your backswing. It delofts the club.

free drop: Drop for which no penalty stroke is incurred, generally within one club length of where the ball was, no closer to the hole.

fried egg: When your ball is partially buried in the sand.

fringe: See *apron*.

front nine: The first half of your round of golf, usually holes 1 through 9.

full swing: The longest swing you make; swinging to the finish.

G

grain: Refers to the direction that the blades of grass are growing. The grass will always grow toward the sun. If you are putting with the grain, the putt will roll faster. If you are putting against the grain, the putt will roll slower. If you are putting across the grain, the ball will usually swerve in the direction that the grass is growing.

green: The putting surface where the hole is located.

green fee: The cost to play a round of golf.

grip: The position in which your hands hold the club. It also refers to the actual part of the club that a player holds during the swing.

grooves: The set of shallow notches on the clubface.

gross score: Actual score shot before a handicap is deducted.

grounding the club: The process of resting the clubhead on the ground behind the ball at address. (You cannot ground the club in a hazard without penalty.)

ground under repair: Area on the course being worked on by the groundskeeper(s), generally marked by white lines, from which you may drop your ball without penalty, just no closer to the hole.

H

hacker: Poor player. Someone who struggles with their game no matter how long they have been playing. (Also, someone with a bad cough!)

handicap: A number that helps measure the skill level of a player. A player with a high handicap will usually shoot a higher score.

hardpan: Very firm turf.

hazard: An obstacle such as sand or water. You cannot ground the club in a hazard without penalty.

head cover: Protection for the clubhead.

heel: The area of the clubface nearest to the shaft of the club.

high side: Area above the hole on a sloping green; pro side. On sloping putts, always aim on the high side (pro side) because a misaimed or mishit putt on the high side may accidentally roll down and into the hole, whereas a ball on the low side will never accidentally roll up and into the hole.

hole: Your target (4.5 inch width). Also used as a verb, such as, "You need to hole this one."

hole-high: Level with the hole.

hole-in-one: When a player's tee shot goes into the hole (every golfer's ultimate goal). Also called *ace*.

hole out: To complete play on a hole.

honor: When you score lowest on the previous hole, you earn the honor (right) to tee off first on the next tee.

hood: Tilting the toe end of the club toward the hole. To hood a club lessens the loft and usually produces a slight draw, a right-to-left shot (for right-handed golfers).

hook: A shot that moves severely on a right-to-left trajectory (for right-handed golfers).

hosel: Curved area where the clubhead connects with the shaft.

hybrid: A golf club that is a cross between an iron and a fairway wood. It looks like a smaller version of a fairway wood. A lot of players are replacing their long irons with hybrids because they are easier to hit.

I

impact: The moment when the club strikes the ball.

impediment: Loose debris that you can remove from around your ball as long as the ball doesn't move.

improve your lie: To move the ball to make a shot easier. This is illegal unless local rules dictate or unless you are a beginner golfer and are playing each round as a practice round. See Chapter 1: Getting Started. (Also, the more you tell your story!)

inside: The area on your side of a line drawn from the ball to the target.

inside-out: The clubhead moves through the impact area on a line to the right of the target (for right-handed golfers).

intended line: The path on which you intend the ball to fly and/or roll from club to target.

interlock grip: Type of grip where the little finger of the right hand is entwined with the index finger of the left (for right-handed golfers).

irons: The clubs other than driver, fairway woods, hybrids, and putter.

J

joy: The reaction you get when you and/or your buddy make a great shot. (Also, possibly the feeling you get when your opponent makes a not-so-great shot.)

K

kill: To hit a long shot, as in, "He killed that one."

L

LPGA: Ladies Professional Golf Association.

lag: A long putt hit with the intent of leaving the ball close to the cup even if it is a bit short of the cup. A putt you may attempt when you fear going past the cup due to the speed of the green.

lateral hazard: Water hazard marked by red stakes and usually parallel to the fairway.

lay-up: Conservatively played shot to avoid possible trouble.

lead side: The side closest to the target (e.g., lead shoulder, lead arm, lead leg).

leading edge: The bottom edge of the clubface.

lie: Where the ball comes to rest on the ground. Also, the angle at which the bottom edge of the clubhead sits relative to the shaft. In addition, when your competitor says he made a four, when he actually made a five—or worse.

line: An imaginary path that you would like your ball to travel on.

links: A seaside course, usually without trees.

lip: The edge of a cup or bunker.

lip out: When the ball touches the edge of the cup but doesn't drop in.

lob: A short, high shot that lands softly.

local knowledge: What the players who play the course a lot know, such as, this putt always breaks toward the clubhouse.

local rules: Set of rules determined by the members, rules committee, or course pro.

loft: The angle of the clubface relative to the ground. Loft is measured in degrees. The greater the loft, the higher and shorter a ball will travel.

long game: Shots hit with long irons and woods.

low handicapper: A good player.

low side: The area below the hole on a sloping green.

M

make: To hole a shot, as in, "He/She needs to make this shot."

makeable: Shot with a good chance of being holed.

mallet: Putter with a deep head.

mark: To indicate the position of the ball with a small, flat object to indicate its position when you lift it. Also, what you put on the ball to personalize it so that you can easily recognize it.

metal wood: Driver or fairway "wood" made of metal.

mis-club: To select the wrong club for the distance.

misread: To choose the wrong line on a putt.

mulligan: Second attempt at a shot without counting a stroke. Illegal shot unless authorized by those hosting a tournament.

municipal course: A course owned by the local government and open to the public.

N

net score: Score for a hole or round after handicap strokes are deducted.

never come up short: It is a proven fact that you miss 100 percent of the shots that come up short.

never up, never in: A saying coined for putts that finish short of the hole.

nineteenth hole: The clubhouse bar. (A place where some golfers truly improve their lie.)

O

obstruction: A manmade object that might interfere with play.

off-center hit: Less than a solid hit.

one-putt: To take only a single putt on a hole.

open clubface: Clubface aligned to the right of the target at address or impact (for right-handed golfers).

open stance: An address position in which the golfer's alignment is to the left of the target (for right-handed golfers).

out-of-bounds: Area outside the boundaries of the course, usually marked with white posts. When a ball finishes out of bounds, the player must return to the original spot and play another ball under penalty of one stroke. He or she thus loses stroke and distance.

outside-in: Swing path in which the clubhead moves into the impact area on a line to the left of the target (for right-handed golfers).

over-club: To use a club that will hit the ball too far.

overlap grip: Type of grip where the little finger of the right hand lies over the index finger of the left hand (for right-handed golfers). Also known as the Vardon grip. This is the most popular of the three grips.

P

par: The par score for a hole is determined by the length and difficulty of the hole. Most courses have two par 5s and two par 3s on each nine. The rest of the holes are par 4s.

PGA: Professional Golfers Association.

pin: The flagstick.

pin-high: Hole-high.

pin placement: The location of the hole on the green.

pitch: A short, high approach shot that doesn't run much on landing.

pivot: The body turn during the swing.

plane: The arc of the swing.

play through: What you should allow the group behind you to do if they are playing faster than your group. See Chapter 22: Golf Etiquette.

plugged lie: When the ball finishes half-buried in the turf or a bunker.

plumb-bob: To line up a putt with one eye closed and the putter held vertically in front of the face.

posture: The overall position of the body and legs in the setup.

pot bunker: A small, steeply faced bunker.

practice green: Place for working on your putting.

preferred lies: Temporary rule that allows you to move the ball to a more favorable position because of abnormally wet conditions.

pro shop: A place where you sign up to start play and where you can buy balls, tees, gloves, hats, shirts, clubs, etc.

provisional ball: If you think your ball may be lost or out of bounds, you may inform your playing partners that you are hitting a provisional ball. You hit the provisional ball from the same spot before looking for the first ball. If the first ball is indeed lost or out of bounds, the second ball is in play, costing you a one-stroke penalty. If the first ball is found, and is not out of bounds, you play it and just pick up the provisional ball.

public course: A golf course open to everyone.

pull: A shot in which the ball starts left of the target and continues to fly in that direction (for right-handed golfers).

punch shot: A low shot hit with the ball back in your stance and with a lower follow-through. On this shot, you don't unhinge your wrists on the follow-through. This shot is used when you need to keep the ball low, under low-hanging branches, etc. This shot is often done with a 7-iron or a 4-iron if you need more distance.

push: A shot in which the ball starts right of the target and continues to fly in that direction (for right-handed golfers).

putt: A stroke made with a putter, which takes place on the green. A putter may also be used from off the green, but the shot is not counted as a putt.

putter: A straight-faced club generally used on the greens.

Q
quitting: Not hitting through a shot. You need to hit through the ball, not to the ball.

R
range: Practice area.

range ball: Generally, a low-quality ball used on a driving range. These balls often have stripes on them. These balls have been paid for by the course owners and, therefore, should be left on the driving range/practice area. Some clubs will actually ban you from the course if you are caught using range balls during play.

reading the green: The process of determining the path on which a putt must travel to the hole. When making this determination, remember that the pace of the putt is the most determining factor.

regulation: The number of strokes needed to reach the green and have two putts left to make par.

release: A term that describes the natural closing of the clubface through and just after impact with the ball.

releasing the club: A phrase describing how the trail hand rolls over the lead hand after impact, indicating a powerful and free swing of the clubhead.

relief: When you drop a ball that was in a penalty area or affected by an obstruction.

rhythm: The fluency of your swing.

roll: The distance a shot travels after landing.

rough: Area of long grass on either side of the fairway or around the green.

round: Eighteen holes of golf.

S

sand trap: Undesirable term for a bunker, for *trap* insinuates that you can't get out.

sandy: Making par after being in a bunker.

scorecard: The card on which the length, par, and rating of each hole is noted, where you record your score after each hole.

scramble: A game in which two or more players tee off, pick the best shot, and then all play their balls within a club length of that shot. The club length cannot be any closer to the hole and the lie must be the same. In other words, if the shot selected was in a bunker, or in the rough, everyone must play from those same conditions. The scramble format is the best format for beginner golfers. Also referred to as *select-a-shot*.

scratch play: No handicaps are used in this type of game.

scratch golfer: A golfer with a zero handicap.

second cut: Second level of rough, higher than the first cut.

select-a-shot: Another name for the scramble format.

semiprivate: A course with members that is also open to the public.

setup: The position of your body in relation to the ball. Always set the clubface up to the ball and then set up to the clubface, with your arms hanging straight down and freely.

shaft: The part of the club that joins the grip to the head.

shag: To retrieve practice balls.

shag bag: A bag designed to retrieve and carry practice balls.

shank: A shot in which the ball is struck from the hosel of the club, causing the ball to fly sharply to the right of the target (for right-handed golfers).

short game: Shots played on and around the green.

shut clubface: Clubface aligned left at address and/or impact (for right-handed golfers). The shot will go to the left of the target (for right-handed golfers).

sidehill lie: Ball either above or below your feet.

sink: To make a putt.

skins: Betting game where the lowest score on a hole wins the pot. If the hole is tied, the money carries over to the next hole.

skull: Shot where the leading edge of the club rather than the clubface strikes the ball, usually leading to a low shot that runs too far.

sleeve of balls: Box of three golf balls.

slice: A shot in which the ball moves from left to right through the air due to sidespin imparted at impact (for right-handed golfers).

slope: A gradual incline. Also, the term for a slope rating, or a number that represents the difficulty of a golf course. The higher the slope number, the more difficult the course.

snap hook: Severe hook.

sole: The bottom of the clubhead. The sole of the club usually rests on the ground at address.

spike mark: Mark on the green made by a golf shoe.

square: When the clubface and stance are aligned perfectly with the target.

square clubface: When the clubface is looking directly down the target line at address and impact.

square grooves: The USGA has banned these from clubfaces. See your golf pro or dealer for clarification.

stance: Position of the feet at address.

starter: Person running the order of play from the first tee.

stimpmeter: Device used to measure the speed of greens.

stroke: The forward movement of the club with the intent to hit the ball. Each stroke counts. Please see *air ball*.

stroke and distance: A penalty in which the golfer must return to the spot from which the last stroke was played, conceding the distance gained, and add one stroke to their score for that hole.

sway: To move excessively away from the ball on the backswing without turning the body—something you don't want to do. On the backswing, you want to turn, not sway.

sweet spot: The optimal hitting area of the clubhead.

swing path: The direction the club is swung. Your swing path will always be along your shoulder line.

swing plane: The angle at which the club shaft travels around the body during a swing.

T

takeaway: Early part of the backswing.

tap-in: Very short putt.

target line: The imaginary line from the golf ball to the target, on which you want the ball to travel.

tee: Wooden or plastic peg on which the ball is set for the first shot on a hole. Also, as a verb, the act of placing your ball on a tee.

tee box: Area in which you must tee your ball, between the tee markers and neither in front of them nor more than two club lengths behind them. While the ball must be teed in this area, the player may stand outside this area when making the shot.

tee time: The time golfers start a round.

tempo: Refers to the speed with which you swing the club.

temporary green: An alternate putting surface used when the permanent green is being renovated or in winter to save wear and tear on the permanent green.

ten-finger grip: Also called *baseball grip*. Type of grip where all ten fingers are on the club. Sometimes used by individuals with small hands.

Texas wedge: Term for a putter when used from off the green.

thin shot: When the leading edge of the clubface strikes the golf ball near its equator. A thin shot will generally fly much lower and farther than normal, with no spin.

three-putt: To take three putts on the green to hole the shot.

tight lie: The ball on bare ground or very short grass.

timing: The pace and sequence of movement in your swing.

toe: The area of the clubface farthest from the shaft of the club.

topped: When the ball is struck on or above the equator. Something you don't want to do.

trail side: The side farther away from the target (e.g., trail arm, trail leg, trail shoulder).

trajectory: The arc on which the ball flies through the air.

trap: See *bunker*.

triple bogey: Three over par on one hole.

turn: To make your way to the back nine holes. Also, the rotation of the upper body during the backswing and the forward swing (downswing and follow-through).

two-handed grip: See *baseball grip*.

U

under-club: To take at least one club less than needed for a given distance.

unplayable lie: Lie from which you can't hit the ball; you may take relief, but you will receive a one-shot penalty.

up and down: To get the ball into the hole in two strokes from off the green.

USGA: United States Golf Association, the ruling body for golf in the United States.

utility wood: A lofted wood (metal) that features a small clubhead designed for advancing shots from the fairway or light rough. Also referred to as *hybrid* or *rescue* club.

V

Vardon grip: See *overlap grip*. The overlap grip is also known as the Vardon grip because Harry Vardon was one of the first great players to use it. This is the most popular of the three grips.

W

waggle: Movement of the clubhead prior to the swing.

water hazard: Body of water that costs you a shot to escape.

wedge: Lofted club used for pitching.

weight shift: The process of transferring your weight from one foot to the other during the swing.

whiff: See *air ball*.

winter rules: See *preferred lies*.

wood: Clubheads on the long clubs (such as fairway woods) which used to be made of persimmon wood. Although the clubheads are no longer made of wood, the term is still quite often used for this type of club.

Y

yips: When a golfer misses short putts because of uncontrollable nerves; when the golfer loses all control of the stroke.